Love, Death, and Exile

Abdul Wahab Al-Bayati

Love, Death, and Exile

Poems Translated from Arabic

by

Bassam K. Frangieh

Bilingual Edition

GEORGETOWN UNIVERSITY PRESS

Washington, D.C.

Georgetown University Press, Washington, D.C.

© 1990 by Bassam K. Frangieh

Printed in the United States of America

10 9 8 7 6 5 4 3 2 1   2004

This book is printed on acid-free paper meeting
the requirements of the American National Standard
for Permanence in Paper for Printed Library Materials.

Library of Congress Cataloging-in-Publication Data

Bayati, `Abd al-Wahhab.

   [Poems. English. Selections]
   Love, death, and exile / Abdul Wahab Al-Bayati ; poems translated
from Arabic by Bassam K. Frangieh.
       p.   cm.
   ISBN 0-87840-217-9. -- ISBN 0-87840-218-7 (pbk.)
   1. Bayati, `Abd al-Wahhab--Translations, English. I. Title.
PJ7816.A92A23   1990
892'.716--dc20   90-20394
                                                            CIP

Contents

Autobiography of the Thief of Fire (1974)   **129**

Shiraz's Moon (1975)   **159**

The Kingdom of Grain (1979)   **233**

Aisha's Orchard (1989)   265

Glossary   309

Preface

On August 3, 1999, Abdul Wahab Al-Bayati, a pioneer of modern Arabic poetry and a leading force in the creation of the Arabic free verse movement, died in Damascus, Syria, his last haven after long years of continuous exile. He had moved from Amman to Damascus earlier the same year after having lived in Jordan since 1992. He suffered a heart attack combined with an asthma attack. *The New York Times* reported on August 5, 1999: "An Iraqi poet who was a major innovator in his art form has died." Other leading international newspapers also reported his death.

I first met Bayati in 1988, in Hammamet, Tunisia, at the Second International Conference on the Dialogue of Cultures and Translation. I spent a few evenings with the poet walking on the shores of the Mediterranean. Then we traveled to Tunis where we spent a week together. This time was of significant personal importance to me. I learned from Bayati far more than I had learned from others during my academic career. I knew I was in the company of a master and a real mentor, both in poetry and life.

I spent the summers of 1995 and 1996 in the company of the poet, in Amman, Jordan. We met in the evenings at al-Finique Gallery, a literary and cultural center. Intellectuals from around the world came to meet Bayati. Journalists, poets, academicians, diplomats, government ministers, politicians, and community and religious leaders would gather around him. He had a likeable, charming personality. Obsessed by the idea of revolutionary change, Bayati stressed that the Arabs, who had achieved a great civilization in the past, could be and must resurrect their civilization. "The Arab leaders are the enemies of their peoples," he maintained. He criticized the tyrant leaders for bringing injustice, oppression, and decay to their citizens and culture. He lent support to people who had been defeated and oppressed. He was a glowing spark from which the Arab masses derive their hope— a much-needed spark in time of despotism, despair, and decline.

In the years that followed, I met with Bayati often. He took me to symposiums, lectures, publishing houses, and bookstores. I wandered with him among the streets and cafes of Arab and Western cities, and we chatted till late hours. He told me stories and revealed secrets. He summed up his life experience and offered it to me on a golden plate. Those were priceless hours and moments of highly concentrated tutelage and profundity, for which I am eternally grateful.

Bayati also introduced me to distinguished political and literary personalities. I found that he was a center of attraction to a widely diverse group of admirers, including sometimes followers of opposing ideologies and political beliefs. During his poetry reading at the University of Pennsylvania in 1991, for example, Sheik Omar Abdulrahman, the convicted mastermind of the 1993 World Trade Center truck bombing, sat in the front row. The blind Muslim cleric had traveled for hours to hear Bayati. On other occasions, I met Iraqi dissidents and other opposition figures when they came to see Bayati. I met personalities from the inner circle of Saddam Hussein, including individuals who would later be captured by the U.S. military. While Bayati had enjoyed the patronage of the late Egyptian President Gamal Abdel Nasser, King Hussein of Jordan, Hafez al-Assad of Syria, he was also a supporter of political groups and individuals who opposed those leaders.

In 1989 Bayati first came to Washington, D.C., to participate in Georgetown University's bicentennial celebration. He came again in February 1991 to celebrate the publication of *Love, Death and Exile*. This visit was of special significance because it was during the first American Gulf War in Iraq. On the morning of the event, the *Washington Post* published an interview with Bayati and that publicity contributed to the larger-than-expected crowd in the auditorium. On that freezing cold day, American and foreign diplomats, Arab ambassadors and Arab communities, news media, students, and faculty came out, many arriving several hours early in order to find seats and to listen to the poet.

During that same visit to the U.S., I accompanied Bayati for a hectic week on a reading tour to Princeton University, the

University of Pennsylvania, and Columbia University, where he again was received as a champion. We traveled by train, stayed in hotels, and met reporters and scholars. We were invited to the homes of many people and spent evenings in New York's fascinating bars and restaurants.

In 1997 I met with Bayati at his favorite restaurant, Al-Yasimeen, in Amman. We had arak, mezza, and dinner, and we talked until midnight. As we left the restaurant, I looked at him and saw an unusual look in his eyes. The poet held me to his chest, held both of my hands, and sadly murmured, "Ashes spread inside me. I feel that this is the last time I will see you." I cried, "Do not say that," but he said, "I am not afraid of death. I am alive inasmuch as I die." When I dropped him off at his home, I turned back hoping to catch one last glimpse. He was still standing there. He was still waving his hand. His face was filled with tears. That was the last time I saw the poet.

In September 1999 I was invited to Georgetown University's Center for Contemporary Arab Studies to speak in honor of the memory of Bayati. It was a sad occasion to eulogize him. I spoke of his life, his recent death, and my vivid memories of time shared with him. I stood behind the podium recalling how, twice before in the same auditorium, he had read his poetry with his sad, proud voice. This time the master was absent.

****

Gail Grella, associate director of Georgetown University Press, informed me of the reprinting of this book. I could not be happier. For me, this book bears the treasures of an important poet, the memory of an honorable man, and the poetic legacy of a nation. Bayati was more than a poet. He was the conscience of his people and a powerful voice for social and political revolution, provocation, and hope. He was very committed and above all, he was a man of great cultural and national importance, a progressive landmark in Arabic heritage and thought. This reprint will ensure the continuity and availability of *Love, Death, and Exile* to readers of the English- and Arabic-speaking worlds.

Introduction

Abdul Wahab Al-Bayati is a renowned contemporary Arab poet and a leader in the free verse movement which began in Iraq in 1948. Together with Nazik Al-Mala'ika and Badr Shakir Al-Sayyab, Al-Bayati led Arabic poetry beyond the constraints of classical Arabic poetical forms, transcending the traditional rhyme schemes and conventional metric patterns which had prevailed for more than fifteen centuries. Yet, even among the pioneers of contemporary Arabic poetry, Al-Bayati is an innovator, for his works depart from classical Arabic poetry in substance as well as structure. Ihsan `Abbas, a major Arab literary critic, commented that, whereas Al-Malaika and Al-Sayyab had "thrown a stone in the water and were pleased with its circular rippling effect, Al-Bayati worked on diverting the course of the water to nurture various seedlings."[1]

This book is the first attempt to introduce the English-speaking world to the work of this acknowledged master of contemporary Arabic poetry. Producing such a book addresses a great need and assumes a great responsibility. Like all works of literary translation, this book seeks to provide greater access to the talents of an acclaimed artist than would otherwise be possible. It is a bridge to a valuable source of insight. At the same time, producing a book of this kind poses weighty challenges and problems. Some of these difficulties—such as preserving both the style and substance of the original work—are inherent in any task of translation. Moreover, the Arabic language is so rich and subtle that it mocks even the most scrupulous attempts to render it effectively in translation.

Al-Bayati's poetry is steeped in mysticism and allusion. This adds a distinctive layer of complexity to his work but also further complicates the task of translation. Moreover, Al-Bayati is a writer whose career spans several decades and whose subjects of interest are remarkably varied. Were Al-Bayati a poet with a smaller output, a shorter career or a narrower range of topics, the choice of what to present, and how to present it, might have been simpler.

This book is a modest attempt to cope with, if not wholly to overcome, these difficulties. It contains fifty-one poems selected from eight collections written over a period of twenty years. The choice of poems partly reflects my personal taste, and to that extent is arbitrary. On the other hand, the poems included in this volume are "representative" in one very important respect: all of them explore the themes of love, death, and exile. None of these themes is treated separately by Al-Bayati, and they all appear frequently in his work. This guided the final selection of poems and determined the title of the volume.

Al-Bayati's poetry is, on its own terms, rich and evocative. Knowing something of his life, however, leads to an even fuller appreciation of his poetry: Al-Bayati's poems are suffused with emotions and reflections drawn from his personal experiences. A close reading of Al-Bayati's poetry strongly suggests that for this poet, perhaps more so than for many others, art and the artist's life are inextricably linked.

One might say that Al-Bayati's early life—viewed in the context of his later experiences and the stature he gained—was rather unremarkable. Born December 19, 1926, in Iraq, Al-Bayati graduated at the age of twenty-four from the Teachers Training College in Baghdad with a degree in Arabic language and literature. In that same year (1950), he took a teaching post and published his first collection of poetry under the title *Mala'ika wa Shayatin* (Angels and Devils).

The year 1953 was a watershed in Al-Bayati's personal and professional life. As contributing editor for the newly founded Iraqi magazine *Al-Thaqafa al-Jadida* (New Culture), he published some of his poems and also criticized the Iraqi monarchy. The undisguised subversive tone of his writing led directly to the closure of the magazine and Al-Bayati's dismissal from his teaching post. Along with other leading intellectuals, Al-Bayati was jailed. Subsequent to his release, he was continually hunted, harrassed and threatened with reincarceration.

Despite the secrecy in which Al-Bayati was compelled to write following his release from prison, his next body of work was a fresh, bold contribution to contemporary Arabic poetry and an equally daring political challenge. This second collection, entitled *Abariq Muhashshamah* (Broken Pitchers, 1954) was genuinely revolutionary both in form and content. Although this volume of poetry earned Al-Bayati wide literary acclaim, the personal costs were tremendous. Al-Bayati was forced to flee Iraq in 1955, leaving behind his wife and family. His itinerant life immediately thereafter led him to take up residence first in Syria, then in Lebanon and Egypt. While in exile, Al-Bayati produced his third collection of poetry, *Al-Majd lil-Atfal wa al-Zaytun* (Glory to Children and Olives, 1956), and his fourth, *Ash`ar fi al-Manfa* (Poems in Exile, 1957).

During the time that he was separated from his family and homeland, Al-Bayati experienced at least one noteworthy stroke of good fortune. This came in the form of an invitation to the Soviet Union by the Organization of Soviet Writers, which Al-Bayati accepted. In Moscow, Al-Bayati met Nazim Hikmet, the well-known Turkish poet-in-exile, who soon became a valued friend and admirer. In a 1959 article, Hikmet praised Al-Bayati's versatility and his ability to blend humanistic and nationalistic concerns in his poetry; and he commended Al-Bayati's spontaneity, simplicity, frankness, and astonishing powers of concentration.[2]

After the July 14, 1958 revolution, which succeeded in deposing the Iraqi monarchy, Al-Bayati returned to Baghdad, where he was appointed director of the translation and research section of the Ministry of Education. The following year he was appointed Iraqi cultural attaché to Moscow. Two years later, he left that post to teach at the Asian Peoples' University in Moscow, where he remained until 1964. After resigning his university post, Al-Bayati moved to Cairo, where he lived for some years before once again assuming the position of cultural attaché, this time in Madrid.

This pattern of changing jobs and shifting residences belies Al-Bayati's consistent devotion to his art. Indeed, Al-Bayati is a prolific poet, having written some twenty collections of poetry in addition to a three-act play, entitled *Muhakamah fi Naysabur* (Trial in Nishapur). He has translated poems by Paul Eluard and Louis Aragon; and he has published studies about them and others as well as a book of prose called *Tajribati al-Shi`riyyah* (My Poetic Experience).

In what ways did this prodigious body of literature and the writer's personal life intertwine? The first point of intersection came in 1944, when Al-Bayati left his village and moved to Baghdad to begin his studies at the Teachers Training College. He immediately came to regard modern urban life and modern Arab cities as cheap replicas of the vibrant cities of ancient civilizations. His revulsion was deeply felt and he concluded that life in the modern Arab city led inexorably to alienation. He wrote contemptuously: "The Tigris-side city which for centuries produced and maintained a great civilization seemed to me dead and finished. I wished it to stay so, to pour its last fragments into a great sea, and there merge and vanish."[3]

Al-Bayati associated the lifestyles of his generation and the physical attributes of the modern city, painting both in images of regret as well as disdain. The poet wrote:

> My generation had lost its character and its real voice and there was no connection between what we studied and what we needed. . . . Such schizophrenia generated a feeling of contradiction between our ideology and reality. . . . We were in need of a fire to burn our reality to give it purity.[4]

Although Al-Bayati keenly appreciated the need to purge and to inspire his generation, he was uncertain of the means to accomplish this purpose. He devoured history books in search of lessons of the past to guide him and his generation away from the misery of oppression under which they languished. He wrote, "History is the type of reading that I love. I did not read it as accumulations of events, but as a wide, humanistic experience of various aspects as well as an embodiment of man's issues that past societies have experienced."[5]

As already mentioned, Al-Bayati was personally and profoundly affected by the suffering of his fellow Arabs. Furthermore, Al-Bayati had himself been victimized by the injustices of the prevailing political structure of Arab states. It is therefore not surprising that Al-Bayati's poetry is written in a spirit of rejection; that he regards it as the poet's duty to resist oppression and partake actively in the struggle for political freedom and social justice. In 1968 he wrote, "I felt at that time that I should write to defend freedom and social justice for the poor. I understand commitment to be that the poet/artist is demanded to his depth to be burned with others when he sees them burning and not to stand on the other side of the bank absorbed in prayer."[6] Thus, for Al-Bayati, poetry which is detached is self-indulgent; art is a social and political mission.

For Al-Bayati, the artist must be prepared to sacrifice himself and to aspire to heroism. The artist's work, moreover, must depict and ennoble such characteristics. Thus, Al-Bayati's rejectionism consists of two elements: a revolt against the stultifying aspects of modern Arab society and a revolt against the conception of the role of the poet as a commentator rather than as a leader in the struggle for freedom. Al-Bayati distinguishes between noble and meaningless death, the former following a life of sacrifice in pursuit of freedom.

Al-Bayati spent most of his life in continuous, sometimes self-imposed, exile. His poetry echoes the triumphs and hardships of his wanderings. Al-Bayati describes himself as the victim of three forms of exile: the exile of existential uncertainty, the exile of physical deprivation, and the exile of rootlessness.[7] In this three-dimensional banishment, the poet faces the ubiquity of death as well as the absence of freedom. Protracted exile traps the poet in a life where physical repatriation might be possible, but psycho-emotional recovery is not. Al-Bayati made just such a point when he wrote, "A poet might still breathe the air of death in his exile, even after his return, and will continue to carry with him his exile within himself."[8]

Despite the unmistakable melancholy and distress that pervades Al-Bayati's poetry, there is a countervailing courage and determination with which he accepts both the past and the future. Candidly, he depicts the poet-revolutionary's life as a kind of lonely sentence. Yet, he emphasizes that the outcome is worth the hardship, and is bound to be a positive one. The following passage highlights this conviction:

> In such a climate full of tension, anxiety and awaiting, I carry every night my cane and depart with the migrant birds, hoping for a miracle to happen. Words work in silence to build up this humanistic spark, this hope, this threat of smoke with which I write my poems.... Here I am searching in this great crowd ... for the legendary historical hero who can change this holy mud and this straw into flame ... into revolution....[9]

It is important to emphasize that, for Al-Bayati, revolutionary change rather than incremental change is necessary to produce a significant improvement in the quality of life in Arab societies. Moreover, Al-Bayati regards revolutionary change in the political structures of Arab societies as the essential precondition for progress in other aspects of life. Hence, neither politics nor revolution are incidental to Al-Bayati's poetry. Revolution and politics are in fact the very hallmark of a substantial portion of Al-Bayati's work. "Lament for the June Sun" is perhaps the best example of what might be called Al-Bayati's "nationalistic poetry." This poem was written after the Arab defeat in 1967 and illustrates the corruption of a nation and its defeat—a defeat which is all the more painful because victory was proclaimed to be close at hand. The poem highlights the deficiencies of the Arab World and its corrupt rulers, who deceived their people by propaganda, cover-ups, and misleading news broadcasts. Al-Bayati incited the Arab World in this moving poem full of poetic images and simple language, rejecting the leaders of that world and calling for their replacement.

Passages such as the one above, which exudes feelings of deep anxiety, might suggest, falsely, that Al-Bayati's poetry is predominantly grim, even fatalistic. In fact, it is replete with examples of his abiding faith. The primary source of his strength is love, whose regenerative power he glorifies again and again in his poetry. Al-Bayati portrays love as the supreme human experience which manifests itself in a variety of forms: love of mother, earth, children, homeland, revolution, and humanity. As if to pay homage to the transcendent quality of love, Al-Bayati rarely depicts it in terms of gender nor mentions the physical appearance of the lover.

For Al-Bayati, love is neither temporary nor proprietary: it exists everywhere and always, and is beyond ownership. Above all, love is an ever-present possibility. Thus, it is the metaphysical companion of the exile: at once his ambition and his consolation. Love makes exile both meaningful and tolerable. In this way, the themes of love and exile are woven together. Love also bears thematically on Al-Bayati's conception of noble death. By providing both reassurance and enticement, love fuels the individual's life struggle and will to resist. In turn, the individual who perseveres in the struggle earns a death which is noble. The recurring appearance of "Aisha" is illustrative of the centrality of love and its consistent meaning in Al-Bayati's poetry. She is the main heroine in Al-Bayati's works and though she assumes a fresh identity in each poem—and often manifests herself in a variety of ways in a single poem—her regular reappearance is an important thread which binds together Al-Bayati's works. Aisha reveals herself to the poet in every place and in everything. She is the lens through which the poet sees himself and the world. However, Aisha appears only to disappear. Every new mask that she wears offers great fulfillment as well as great disappointment, for Aisha is unattainable. Each successive appearance is ultimately a reminder of her imminent departure. Thus, when Aisha appears—only to depart again—the poet's tragedy deepens and love comes to be associated with suffering.[10]

Perhaps the most striking technical feature of Al-Bayati's poetry (which the discussion of Aisha's polymorphous appearances has already partially uncovered) is his liberal use of what might be termed "poetic masks." That is to say, Al-Bayati introduces poetic figures or characters whose attributes creatively reflect those Al-Bayati finds admirable. The features inscribed on these "masks" are drawn from legends and from history. This technique offers several advantages to the poet. First, it enables Al-Bayati to create an existence ostensibly independent of, yet in actual fact, intimately related to his own existence. The mask in effect creates an artificial divide between the artist and his art. Second and relatedly, it allows Al-Bayati to avoid the pitfalls of didacticism. The lessons of his own experiences are lived by his characters, not preached in his own voice. Third, the "mask" allows Al-Bayati to treat the dialectic of life/death/resurrection in a variety of ways. Substituting one "mask" for another, Al-Bayati is better able to illustrate the passage from struggle to triumph in its infinite forms.

Several of the poems contained in this volume are among Al-Bayati's most elegant yet most complex pieces. Thus, while they might be potentially the most appealing, they are also among the most inaccessible of his works. This is even more likely to be the case for non-Arabic speakers unacquainted with the literary allusions which give certain poems their essential meaning. In order to enable the reader to gain a fuller enjoyment and appreciation of these poems, it might be helpful to comment briefly on two poems which are particularly sophisticated in this respect, namely, "The Magus" and "Eye of the Sun."

In "The Magus," Al-Bayati speaks through several voices: the voice of a child, that of a mystic, and that of a disillusioned man in his twilight years. Initially, the child delights in the world around him and in his experiences. Images of flowers and butterflies reveal the child's world as one of beauty and love. Yet, as the poem progresses, the child is despoiled of his youth; the beauty around him vanishes. With all that had been familiar and therefore comforting gone, the child's mood is transformed. At only ten years of age, he feels alienated and alone. His next important discovery is that life itself is absurd. Following from this he learns that the passage to salvation lies through suffering in pursuit of supreme love and death. This painful process of discovery is reminiscent of the torture of Al-Hallaj and the sufferings of Al-Khayyam. What stands out as Al-Bayati's trademark is his character's determination to overcome his condition. Although the poem ends in winter and death, Al-Bayati places emphasis on the character's sincerity and faithfulness. To the end, the "child" neither seeks a return to his childhood nor begs for love. Rather, he adheres to his commitment to rid society of corruption and bring a new spring to those around him.[11]

In his poem, "Eye of the Sun," Al-Bayati speaks through Ibn `Arabi, the mystic poet, who had dedicated a volume of poetry to his lover entitled *Turjuman al-Ashwaq* (Translation of Desires). Al-Bayati recreates the relationship between Ibn `Arabi and his beloved, Al-Nizam, who is nicknamed `Ain al Shams (Eye of the Sun). Al-Bayati substitutes Damascus for Mecca and Qasyun for Mount `Arafat. He then depicts Ibn `Arabi in his last days in Damascus, where he sees his beautiful young Al-Nizam everywhere and in everything. Mirroring Ibn `Arabi's poetic technique, Al-Bayati employs a number of symbols: a gazelle to represent the beloved, the green moon to stand for hope, blackness (shadows) as a sign of the oppression which covers the earth, and lightning as divine revelation. The vivid image of the gazelle running in the dark across the desert functions as this poem's version of Al-Bayati's recurring theme: love is the means to salvation.

The gazelle, which in Ibn `Arabi's poetry means God's secrets and light, survives people's cruelty and ignorance and acts as an intermediary for revelation. The gazelle is "hunted" and "tortured"—but not killed—by the ignorant who fail to recognize the secrets and truths which she bears. The gazelle vanishes, but she does not die. Meanwhile, the poet alone knows her true worth, and searches vainly for the gazelle. Though confined to the "real" (and therefore ugly) world and separated from the beloved, the poet nonetheless comes to realize that through sacrifice (martyrdom), a reunion with the beloved is indeed possible. Thus, the poem continues even after Al-Bayati's "Ibn `Arabi" dies. His "Ibn `Arabi" lives after death: through hardship and self-sacrifice he is transfigured. The mystic state of utopian innocence and purity which characterizes the end of the poem is Al-Bayati's idealized conception of the triumph which follows a life of painful and sincere struggle.[12]

It would perhaps be a disservice both to Al-Bayati and to the reader to offer further comment on the content of the poems in this volume. Better to allow those who are privileged—as I have been—to read the poems to discover to their own delight the beauty and meaning of Al-Bayati's works. I hope that the selections I have made, the translations I have offered, and the few remarks with which I have begun this volume will have made that process slightly easier and also more fulfilling.

Bassam K. Frangieh

Washington, D.C.
September, 1990

Notes

1. `Abbas, Ihsan. *Ittijahat al-Shi`r al-`Arabi al-Mu`asir* (Directions of Contemporary Arabic Poetry). Kuwait: Al-Majlis al-Watani lil-Thaqafah wa al-Funun wa al-Adab, 1978, p. 56.

2. The article is printed in Al-Bayati's collection, *`Ishrun Qasidah Min Birlin* (Twenty Poems from Berlin). Beirut: Dar al-`Awdah, 1970, pp. 5-15.

3. Al-Bayati, Abdul Wahab. *Tajribati al-Shi`riyyah* (My Poetic Experience). Beirut: Manshurat Nizar Qabbani, 1968, p. 12.

4. Ibid.

5. Ibid., p. 16.

6. Ibid., p. 21.

7. Ibid., p. 22.

8. Ibid., p. 23.

9. Ibid., pp. 44-45.

10. Subhi, Muhyi al-Din. *Al-Ru'yah fi Shi`r al-Bayati* (Vision in Al-Bayati's Poetry). Baghdad: Dar al-Shu'un al-Thaqafiya al-`Ammah, 1987. pp. 265-67.

11. Ibid., pp. 263-65.

12. Ibid., pp. 309-19.

القديس

إلى الدكتور لويس عوض

أُصيبَ بالكآبة
ومرضِ الكتابة
والأرقِ المزمنِ والإحساسِ بالموتِ
وبالإحباط والتعاسة
وعندما اشتدَّ عليه المرضُ اللعينُ
فاضت روحهُ
تُوِّجَ بالقداسة

عبد الوهاب البياتي

The Saint

(for Lewis `Awad)

Struck with sadness
Compelled to write
Endless sleeplessness
Intimations of death,
Defeat and misery.
When the cursed sickness
Took the upper hand
His soul took flight
To his seat of holiness.

عيون الكلاب الميتة
(١٩٦٩)

14

The Eyes of the Dead Dogs

(1969)

- *The City*
- *Lament for the June Sun*
- *Something About Happiness*

المدينة

— ١ —

وعندما تعرت المدينة
رأيت في عيونها الحزينة :
مباذل الساسة واللصوص والبياذق
رأيت في عيونها : المشانق
تُنصب والسجون والمحارق
والحزن والضياع والدخان
رأيتُ في عيونها : الانسانْ
يُلصق مثل طابع البريدْ
في أيما شيء
رأيتُ : الدم والجريمةْ
وعلبَ الكبريت والقديد
رأيت في عيونها : الطفولة اليتيمة
ضائعة تبحث في المزابلْ
عن عظمةٍ
عن قمر يموتُ
فوق جثث المنازل
رأيت : انسان الغد المعروض في واجهة المخازن
وقطع النقود والمداخن
مُجللاً بالحزن والسواد

The City

I

When the city undressed herself
I saw in her sad eyes:
The shabbiness of the leaders, thieves, and pawns.
I saw in her eyes:
The gallows, the prisons, and the incinerators,
The sadness, the confusion, and the smoke.
I saw in her eyes:
All men
Glued like postage stamps
On everything.
I saw:
The blood and the crime
And the match boxes and the meat tins.
I saw in her eyes:
The orphan childhood
Wandering, searching in the garbage dumps
For a bone
For a moon dying
Upon the corpses of houses.
I saw: the man of tomorrow
Displayed in the storefronts,
On the coins and in the chimneys,
Clothed in sorrow and blackness

مكبلاً يبصق في عيونه : الشرطيُّ
واللوطيُّ
والقوَّاد
رأيت في عيونها الحزينة :
حدائق الرماد
غارقةً في الظل والسكينةْ

— ٢ —

وعندما غطى المساء عُريَها
وخيّم الصمتُ على بيوتها العمياء ْ
تأوهت
وابتسمت رغم شحوب الداء
وأشرقت عيونها السوداء بالطيبة والصفاء

□   □   □

The policemen, the sodomites, and the pimps
Spitting in his eyes
As he lay shackled.
I saw in her sad eyes:
The gardens of ashes
Drowned in shadow and stillness.

II

When the evening covered her nudity
And the silence enveloped her blind houses,
She sighed
And smiled despite the pallor of her sickness.
Her black eyes shone with goodness and purity.

* * *

بكائية الى شمس حزيران

الى ذكرى زكي الارسوزي

طحنتنا في مقاهي الشرقِ
حربُ الكلماتْ
والسيوفُ الخشبيةْ
والأكاذيبُ
وفرسانُ الهواء
نحن لم نقتل بعيراً
أو قطاة
لم نُجرب لعبةَ الموتِ،
ولم نلعب مع الفرسانِ
أو نرهن الى الموت جوادْ
نحن لم نجعل من الجرح دواة
ومن الحبر دماً
فوق حصاة
شغلتنا الترهات
فقتلنا بعضنا بعضاً
وها نحن فُتات
في مقاهي الشرقِ
نصطاد الذبابْ
نرتدي أقنعة الأحياء،
في مزبلة التاريخ،
أشباه رجال

20

Lament for the June Sun

(in memory of Zaki Al-Arsuzi)

We were ground in the coffeehouses of the East by
War of words
Wooden swords
Lies and empty heroes.
We did not kill a camel or a grouse
We did not try the game of death
We did not play with knights or give up even one horse
We did not make an inkwell from the wound
We did not make blood from ink
Upon a single pebble.
Trivia preoccupied us
We killed each other and now we are crumbs
In the coffeehouses of the East we swat at flies
We wear the masks of living people
We are half men
In the garbage dump of history.

لم نُعلق جرساً
في ذيل هر أو حمارْ
أو نَقُلْ للأعور الدجالِ :
لم لذتَ
بأذيال الفرار
نحن جيل الموت بالمجان،
جيل الصدقات
هزمتنا في مقاهي الشرقِ
حربُ الكلماتْ
والطواويس التي تختالُ
في ساحاتٍ
موت الكبرياء
ومقالات الذيول الأدعياء
آه لَطّخْ هذه الصفحةَ،
هذا الخبر الكاذبْ،
ياسارق قوت الفقراء
وحذاء الأمراء
بدم الصدق
وَمُتْ مثل فقاعات الهواء
لم نعُدْ نقوى على لعق الأكاذيب
وتحبير الهُراء
واجترار الترهات
نحن جيل الموت بالمجان،
جيل الصدقات

We did not hang a bell on the tail of a cat or a donkey
We did not ask the blind deceiver: Why did you flee?
We are the generation of meaningless death
The recipients of alms.
In the coffeehouses of the East we were defeated by
The war of words
The peacocks who strut in the halls where pride is dead, and
The essays of the obedient hacks.
O you thief of the poor's food and the princes' shoes,
Stain this page, this false news
With the blood of truth, and
Die like bubbles in the air.
We can no longer swallow lies
Or write the nonsense
Or engage in idle talk
We are the generation of meaningless death
The recipients of alms.

لم نمُتْ يوماً
ولم نُولَد
ولم نعرف عذاب الشهداء
فلماذا تركونا في العراء؟
يا المي
للطيور الجارحات
نرتدي أسمال موتانا،
ونبكي في حياء
آه لم تترك على عورتنا
شمسُ حزيرانَ رداءْ
ولماذا تركونا للكلاب؟
جيفاً دون صلاة
حاملين الوطن المصلوب في كفٍ
وفي الاخرى التراب
آه لا تطرد عن الجرح الذباب
فجراحي فمُ «أيوبَ»
وآلامي انتظار
ودم يطلب ثار
يا اله الكادحين الفقراء
نحن لم نُهزَمْ
ولكن الطواويس الكبار
هُزموا هُمْ وحدهمْ،
من قبل أن ينفخ ديـــار بنار

*

We neither died one day nor were born
Nor knew the anguish of heroes.
Why did they leave us naked
O my God
For the predatory birds
Wearing the tatters of our dead and crying in shame?
Ah, the sun of June
Left our genitals naked.
Why did they leave us for the dogs
Corpses without prayer
Carrying the crucified nation in one hand and dust in the other?
Don't brush the flies from the wound
My wounds are the mouth of Job
My pains are patience waiting
And blood seeking revenge.
O Lord of the poor workers
We were not defeated
The giant peacocks alone were defeated
Quicker than the flicker of a flame.

آه ياقبر حكيم نام بين الفقراء
صامتاً يلبس أكفان الحداد
صامتاً يُشعل نار
قُم تحدَّث :
نحن موتى
نحن جيل الموت بالمجان
جيل الصدقات

□   □   □

O grave of the wise man
Who slept among the poor,
Silent, wearing the shroud of mourning
Silent, sparking a fire
Rise up and speak:
We are dead
We are the generation of meaningless death
We are the recipients of alms.

* * *

شيء عن السعادة

كذبوا، ان السعادةً
يامحمدْ
لاتُباغ
فالجرائد
كتبتْ : ان السماء
أمطرت في ليلة الأمس ضفادع
ياصديقي، سرقوا منك السعادة
خدعوكَ
عذبوكَ
صلبوكَ
في حبال الكلمات
ليقولوا عنك : مات
ليبيعوك مكاناً في السماء
آه ماجدوى البكاء
أنا خجلانُ محمد
فالضفادع
سرقت منا السعادة
وأنا رغم العذاب
في طريق الشمس سائر

٭

Something About Happiness

They lied.
Happiness,
O Muhammed,
Is not for sale.
The newspapers
Wrote that the sky
Rained frogs last night.
O my friend,
They stole happiness from you
They deceived you,
Tortured you,
Crucified you
In the snare of words
In order to say:
He died
To sell you a place in the sky.
Ah, crying is in vain
I am ashamed, Muhammed,
The frogs
Stole happiness from us,
Yet in spite of the suffering, I am
On the road to the sun, marching.

*

زرعوا الليل خناجرْ
وكلاب

٭

إن سقف الليل ينهار عليهم
فتمرد !
يا محمد !
فتمرد !
وحذارٍ أن تخون

◻   ◻   ◻

They planted the night with daggers
And dogs.

*

The night's ceiling is collapsing upon them.
So, revolt!
O Muhammed,
Revolt!
But do not betray.

* * *

الكتابة على الطين
(١٩٧٠)

- المجوسي
- كابوس الليل والنهار
- مرثية إلى المدينة التي لم تولد
- ثلاث رسوم مائية

Writing on Clay

(1970)

- *The Magus*
- *The Nightmare of Night and Day*
- *Elegy to the Unborn City*
- *Three Watercolors*

المجــوســي

‐ ١ ‐

سكبوا فوق ثيابي الخمرَ، عربدتُ من الحب
وراقصتُ الفراشات وعانقتُ الزهور
منحوني عندليباً وقمر
ومرايا وتعاو يذَ وقطرات مطر
وأنا لم أتعدّ العاشرة
فلماذا عندليب الحبّ طار؟
والمرايا صدئت فوق الجدار
ولماذا استرجعوا مني القمر
والتعاو يذ وَقطرات المطر
عندما قلبي على أرصفة الليل انكسر

‐ ٢ ‐

المجوسي من الشرفة للجار يقول :
يالها من بنت كلبه
هذه الدنيا التي تُشبعنا موتاً وغربه
كان قلبي مثل شحاذ على الابواب يستجدي المحبه
وأنا لم أتعدّ العاشرة

34

The Magus

I

They spilled wine over my clothing
I was quarrelsome from love
And danced with the butterflies,
Embraced the flowers.
They gave me a nightingale and a moon,
Mirrors, magic charms, and drops of rain
When I was not even ten
Why did the nightingale of love fly away?
And why did the mirrors rust
Upon the wall?
Why did they take back the moon
The magic charms and the drops of rain?
When my heart was broken into pieces
On the sidewalks of the night?

II

From the balcony
The Magus says to his neighbor:
This son-of-a-bitch life
Fills us with death and exile!
My heart was a beggar,
Pleading at the doors of love
When I wasn't even ten

فلماذا أغلقوا الأبواب في وجهي ؟
لماذا عندليب الحبّ طار؟
عندما مات النهار

— ٣ —

ساحر يأتي مع الليل وسحر لايدوم
باطل ماتكتب الريح على السور وماقالت الى البحر النجوم
كان حبي لك موتاً ورحيل
ياوصايا النار، يا أرض سدوم

— ٤ —

وجدوه عند باب البيت في الفجر قتيل
وعلى جبهته جرح صغير وقمر
وتعاو يذُ وقطراتُ مطر

□   □   □

Why did they shut the doors in my face?
And why did the nightingale of love fly away
When the day died?

III

A magician comes with the night but
His magic doesn't last
It is false
What the wind writes on the walls
And what the stars say to the sea
My love for you was death and voyage,
O commandments of fire, O land of the sodomites!

IV

They found him murdered at dawn
In front of the house's gate
On his forehead a small wound and a moon,
Magic charms, and drops of rain.

* * *

كابوس الليل والنهار

تحلم الأرض بميلاد نبيّ يملأُ الآفاق عدلاً
تحلم الأرض بميلاد الفضول
وأنا أحمل في الشارع جثة
لأواريها ، اذا ماهبط الليل ، بمبغى أو حديقة
وبمقهى أو بخمارة نور
مُخفياً وجهي عن الله وعنكِ
خجلاً سكرانَ أبكي
وتقول الأغنية—
بعد أن عُبّىء صوت العندليب
والمغني وهو للشمس يغني — في اسطوانه
بعد أن بيعت ودبَّ الشيب في رأس المغني
ودم الوردة فوق الأفق سال
ماالذي كانت تقول الأغنية ؟
والعصافير على أرصفة الليل تموت
والنبي المُنتظر
نائماً ما زال في الغار وما زال المطر
فوق جدران البيوت الهرمه
وسطوح المدن الحبلى واعلانات سمساري البيوت
بدم يكتب ميلاد وموت الكلمة
وأنا أحمل في الشارع جثه
مخفياً وجهي عن الله وعنكِ
ليَم تبكي ؟

The Nightmare of Night and Day

While earth dreams of the birth of a prophet
Who will fill the horizons with justice
And of the birth of the seasons,
I carry a corpse in the streets
At nightfall
I will bury it in a brothel or a park
Or in a coffeehouse or a tavern of light,
Hiding my face from God and you,
Ashamed, and drunk, I cry
The song says —
After the voices of the nightingale
And the singer singing to the sun —
Were captured in a record
The record was sold,
And the grey hairs crawled into the singer's head
And the blood of the rose flew upon the horizon,
But what did the song say?
The birds on the sidewalks of the night died
And the awaited prophet
Was still sleeping in the cave
And the rain still fell
Upon the walls of the houses
And the roofs of the pregnant cities
And on the real estate advertisements
The awaited prophet was writing
The birth and death of the word in blood
While I carried a corpse in the street,
Hiding my face from God and you
Why do you cry?

أيها النهر الخزافي الذي يرضع أثداء المدينة
حاملاً أوساخها نحو البحار
والخيول الميته
وحطام العربات
وأنا أشهد ميلاد النهار
في عيون القطط المحتضره
بعد أن عُبىء صوت العندليب
والمغني وهو للشمس يغني ــ في اسطوانه
كانت الجثةُ تبكي
وأنا أبحث في الشارع عنكِ
والتقينا بعد أن مات النهار
ثم جاء الليل من بعد النهار
ونهار آخر بعد النهار
وتدور الاسطوانه
ومغنيها بصوت شرخته السنوات
لاهثاً يجري وراء الظلمات

...   .

...   .

ما الذي كانت تقول الأغنية ؟
ما الذي كانت تقول الأغنية ؟

□   □   □

O you mythical river that sucks
The breasts of the city,
Carrying towards the seas, its filth
And the dead horses
And the wreckage of the chariots
I witness the birth of the day
In the eyes of the dying cats
After the voices of the nightingale
And the singer singing for the sun
Were captured in a record
While I was searching for you in the streets
The corpse was crying
We met after the day died
Then the night came after the day
And another day came after the day
And the record turned,
And its singer with a voice cracked by the years,
Gasped, running behind the darkness
....
....
But what did the song say?
What did the song say?

* * *

مرثية الى المدينة التي لم تولد

تطن بالناس و بالذباب
وُلدتُ فيها وتعلمتُ على أسوارها الغربة والتجواب
والحب والموت ومنفى الفقر في عالمها السفليِّ والأ بواب
علَّمني فيها أبي: قراءة الأنهار
والنار والسحاب والسراب
والرفض والاصرار
علَّمني : الابحار
والحزن والطواف
حول بيوت أولياء الله
بحثاً عن النور وعن دفء ربيع لم يجيء بعدُ
ومازال ببطن الأرض والأصداف
منتظراً نبوءة العرّاف
علَّمني فيها : انتظار الليل والنهار
والبحث في خريطة العالم عن مدينةْ
مسحورة دفينه
تشبهها في لون عينيها وفي ضحكتها الحزينة
لكنها لا ترتدي الاسمال
وَخِرقَ المهرج الجوّال
ولا يطن صيفها بالناس والذباب

□   □   □

Elegy to the Unborn City

Buzzing with people and flies,
I was born in it, and
On its walls I learned exile and wandering,
Love and death and the isolation of poverty
In its underworld and at its gates.
In it my father taught me to navigate and to read:
The rivers, the fires, the clouds, and the mirage
He taught me to know sadness, rebellion, and perseverance
To sail, and to circle the houses of the saints of god,
Searching for the light and the warmth of a future spring
Which still lives at the bottom of the earth
And in the sea shells,
Awaiting the prophecy of a fortune teller.
In it he taught me to wait for the night and the day
And to search for a hidden, enchanted city
On the map of the world
Similar to my city
In the color of its eyes and in its sad laugh,
But not wearing
The tatters of the wandering clown,
Nor does its summer buzz with people and flies.

* * *

ثلاث رسوم مائية

― ١ ―

تتفجر الأضواء عبر مخاضة اللون القتيل على الجدار
رحلتُ ولكن الربيع على الوسادة لايزال
مستلقياً عريان تغمره الظلال
رحلتُ كما رحل النهار
لكنه رش النجوم على النوافذ وهي لم تترك سوى
هذا الرماد

ياسندبادُ ألم تكن ― ياسندباد
تغزو المرافىء والقلوب مُخَلِّفاً في كل ميناءٍ
سفينك في اشتعال

فعلام أطفأت الذبال ؟
ورحلتُ أو رحلتْ ــ كما ارتحل المجوس الى الجبال
وعلام كفّ القلبُ في صمت البحار عن الحوار ؟
وماتت المدن البعيدة والمرافىء والنهار ؟
ووجوه حوريات أعماق البحار ؟

― ٢ ―

ماذا يقول العندليب ؟
للسائرين بنومهم ، ماذا يقول العندليب ؟

Three Watercolors

I

The light exploded over
The churning of the assassinated color on the walls
She departed, but spring remained on the pillow,
Reclining naked, covered by shadows
She departed like the day,
But it sprinkled stars on the windows
And she left only ashes.
O Sinbad,
Didn't you ever invade harbors and hearts
Leaving your blazing ships at each port?
So why did you extinguish their fire
And why did you or she depart
Like the Magi for the mountains?
Why did the heart stop talking in the silence of the seas?
Why did the distant cities, the harbors, and the day die
And the faces of the nymphs
At the bottom of the seas?

II

And what does the nightingale say for the sleepwalker?
What does the nightingale say?

غدرت بك الألوان والدنيا كما غدرت
بعاشقها لعوب
ورحلت وَارتحلتُ كما ارتحل المجوس
بلا طقوس
هرباً من الظلمات والأموات والليل الطويل
ومخاضة اللون القتيل
فعلام كاشفت الوجود ؟
ووقعت في شرك الوجود
متفجراً من داخل الأشياء ، منفياً تموت
ومدمراً في كل ميناء حياتك في غياب الآخرين
ومطارداً للنور في هذا الكمين
يا أيها الوثنيُ ، ياقلبي الحزين

— ٣ —

تتنكرين بزي ساحرة وفي ورق الخريف أميرةٌ
تتقنَّعين
وتضاجعينَ البرق في قاع البحار وفي الجبال
غزالةٌ تتراكضين
وعلى وجوه العاشقين فراشةً تتراقصين
ومع الطيور تهاجرين
وعلى زجاج نوافذ المقهى وفي ليل الشوارع تشعلين
نار الحنين
وعلى سطوح منازل المدن البعيدة تمطرين

The colors and life betrayed you
Like a flirtatious woman betrays her lover.
You and she departed
Like the Magi departed,
Without rituals,
Fleeing the darkness, the dead, and the long night
And the churning of the murdered colors.
Why did you reveal yourself to your existence
Falling into its snare?
Exploding inside things, exiled, dying
And in the absence of the others,
Destroying your life in each harbor,
Driving away light in this ambush
Oh you pagan,
Oh my sad heart.

III

A sorceress
In the autumn leaves,
You are disguised as a princess,
Making love to the lightning in the depths of the seas,
In the mountains you are a running gazelle
You are a dancing butterfly on the faces of the lovers
You migrate with the birds
On the glass of the cafe windows
And in the night streets
You ignite the fire of yearning
And on the roofs of the distant city houses,
You rain

وأنا أموت كقطرة المطر الحزين
متنكراً بقناع أعياد الطفولة أو عناد الرافضين
متحسساً رأسي وأنت مع القوافل ترحلين
وتمارسين السحر في الواحات كاهنةً
وفي سعف النخيل تلوّحين

للسائرين بنومهم والهائمين
وتضاجعين الميتين
وتهوّمين وتختفين
والى بلادك ترحلين
وأنا أموت كقطرة المطر الحزين
على وجوه العابرين

□   □   □

I die like a drop of sad rain,
Disguised in a mask of childhood holidays and stubbornness
Feeling my head
While you leave with the caravans,
Practicing magic in the oasis like a priestess,
Waving the air with palm branches
For the wanderers and the sleepwalkers,
Making love to the dead
And disappear, falling asleep.
You depart to your country
I die like a drop of sad rain
Upon the faces of the passersby.

* * *

قصائد حب
على بوابات العالم السبع
(1971)

50

Love Poems at the
Seven Gates of the World

(1971)

عين الشمس

— ١ —

أحمل قاسيون

غزالة تعدو وراء القمر الاخضر في الديجور

ووردة أرشق فيها فرس المحبوب

وحملاً يثغو وأبجدية

أنظمُهُ قصيدة ، فترتمي دمشق في ذراعه قلادة من نور

أحمل قاسيون

تفاحة أقضمها

وصورة أضمها

تحت قميص الصوف

أكلم العصفور

و بردى المسحور

فكل إسم شـارد ووارد أذكـره : عـنها أكني واسمها أعني

وكل دار في الضحى أندبها : فدارها أعني

توحّــد الواحد في الكل

والظل في الظل

وولد العالم من بعدي ومن قبلي

Eye of the Sun

I

I carry Qasyun
A gazelle running behind the green moon in the dark,
A rose thrown on the steed of the lover,
A bleating lamb,
An alphabet,
I transform it into a poem
So Damascus will fall into its arms,
A necklace made of light.
I carry Qasyun
An apple I bite,
A picture I clutch
Under my wool shirt.
I speak to the birds
And to Barada the enchanted
Whatever name I mention, is her name I am calling
Every house I lament in the morning is her house.
The one is unified with the all
The shadow with the shadow
The world was born before me
And will remain after me.

كلمني السيد والعاشق والمملوك
والبرق والسحابة
والقطب والمريدْ
وصاحب الجلالةْ
أهدى إليَّ بعد أن كاشفني غزالة
لكنني أطلقتها تعدو وراء النور في مدائن الأعماق
فاصطادها الأغراب وهي في مراعي الوطن المفقود
فسلخوها قبل أن تذبح أو تموت
وصنعوا من جلدها ربابة ووتراً لعود
وها أنا أنشده: فتورق الأشجار في الليل و يبكي
عندليب الريح

وعاشقات بردى المسحور
والسيد المصلوب فوق السور

تقودني أعمى إلى منفاي : عينُ الشمس

تملكتني مثلما امتلكتُها تحت سماء الشرق
وهبتها ووهبتني وردة ونحن في مملكة الرب نصلي
في انتظار البرق

II

The Lord, the lover, the slave,
The lightning and the cloud,
The master and the disciple spoke to me.
And the almighty,
After lifting the clouds,
Gave me a gazelle,
But I set her free to run behind the light
In the cities of the depths.
Strangers hunted her in the meadows of the lost nation
And skinned her alive
From her skin they made a rebak and a lute string
I pluck.
In the night the trees sprout leaves
The nightingale of the wind weeps
With the lovers of Barada the enchanted
And the Lord crucified upon the wall.

III

She leads me blind into exile: eye of the sun.

IV

She possessed me as I possessed her under the sky of the East
I gave her a rose, she gave me a rose:
We prayed in the kingdom of the Lord,
Waiting for the lightning.

لكنها عادت إلى دمشق°
مع العصافير ونور الفجر
تاركة مملوكها في النفي
عبداً طروباً آبقاً مهيأ للبيع
وميتاً وحي
يرسم في دفاتر الماء وفوق الرمل
جبينها الطفل وعينيها وومض البرق عبر الليل
وعالماً يموت أو يولد قبل صيحة الموت أو الميلاد

— ٥ —

أيتها الأرض التي تعفنت فيها لحوم الخيل والنساء
وجثث الأفكار
أيتها السنابل العجفاء
هذا أوان الموت والحصاد

— ٦ —

قريبة دمشق
بعيدة دمشق
من يوقف النزيف في ذاكرة المحكوم بالاعدام قبل الشنق؟
و يرتدي عباءة الولي والشهيد ؟
و يصطلي مثلي بنار الشوق؟
أيتها المدينة الصبية
أيتها النبية

But she returned to Damascus
With the birds and the light of the dawn,
Leaving her slave in exile:
Joyful fugitive prepared for sale
Dead and alive,
Drawing on books of water and on the sand
Her child's brow, her eyes
The flash of the lightning across the night
And a world that dies or is born before the cry
Of death or birth.

V

O land full of putrid flesh of horses and women and
The corpses of ideas
O lean ears of grain
This is the time of death and harvest.

VI

Damascus is near.
Damascus is far.
Who will stop the bleeding in the memory of the man
Destined to be hanged?
Who will wear the robe of the saint and the martyr?
Who will burn like me in the fire of yearning?
O young city
O prophetess

أكُتِبَ الفراق والموت علينا ؟ كُتِبَ الترحال
في هذه الأرض التي لا ماء ، لاعشب بها ، لانار
غير لحوم الخيل والنساء
وجثث الأفكار

— ٧ —

لا تقترب ممنوع
فهذه الأرض إذا أحببت فيها حَكَمَ القانون
عليك بالجنون

— ٨ —

عدت إلى دمشق بعد الموت
أحمل قاسيون
أعيده إليها
مقبلاً يديها
فهذه الأرض التي تحدها السماء والصحراء
والبحر والسماء
طاردني أمواتها وأغلقوا عليَّ باب القبر
وحاصروا دمشق
وأوغروا عليّ صدر صاحب الجلالة
من بعد أن كاشفني وذبحوا الغزالة
لكنني أفلتُ من حصارهم وعُدت

Is our fate separation and death?
Is it wandering?
In this land of no water, no pasture, no fire
Only the flesh of horses and women
And the corpses of ideas.

VII

Don't approach. It is forbidden:
If you love in this land
The law will convict you of madness.

VIII

I returned to Damascus after death,
Carrying Qasyun,
Returning it to her,
Kissing her hands.
For this land, bound by sky and desert,
By sky and sea,
Its dead chased me
And locked the tomb's door on me,
Besieging Damascus.
They turned the almighty against me
After he lifted the clouds and they slaughtered the gazelle.
But I escaped their siege and returned,

أحمل قاسيون
تفاحة أقضمها
وصورة أضمها
تحت قميص الصوف
من يوقف النزيف ؟
وكل مانحبه يرحل أو يموت
يا سفن الصمت و يادفاتر الماء وقبض الريح
موعدنا : ولادة أخرى وعصر قادم جديد
يسقط عن وجهي وعن وجهك فيه الظل والقناع
وتسقط الأسوار

□   □   □

Carrying Qasyun
An apple I bite,
A picture I clutch
Under my wool shirt.
Who will stop the bleeding?
All that we love departs or dies.
O ships of silence, books of water, handfuls of wind
We will meet in another birth, in a new era
When from my face and your face
The shadow and the mask will fall
And the walls will collapse.

* * *

عـن وضـاح اليمـن
والحب والموت

— ١ —

يصعد من مدائن السحر ومن كهوفها : وضاح
متوجاً بقمر الموت ونار نيزك . يسقط في الصحراء
تحمله إلى الشآم عندليباً برتقالياً مع القوافل : السعلاة
وريشة حمراء
ينفخها الساحر في الهواء
يكتب فيها رقيةً لسيدات مدن الرياح
وكلمات الحجر الساقط في الآبار
ورقصات النار
ينفخها في مجلس الخليفة
فتستحيل تارة قصيدة
وتارة لؤلؤة عذراء
تسقط عند قدميْ وضاح
يحملها إلى السرير امرأة تضج بالأهواء
تمارس الحب مع الليل وضوء القمر المجنون
تهذي، تغني، تنتهي من حيث لا تبدأ، تستعيد
تعود عذراء على سريرها خجلى من الليل
وضوء القمر المجنون
تفتح عينيها على رماد نار نيزك يسقط في الصحراء

About Waddah of Yemen —
Love and Death

I

From the cities of magic and the caves: Waddah arises,
Crowned by the moon of death and the fire of a shooting star,
Falling into the desert,
Carried like an orange nightingale
By the ogress with the caravans
To Syria.
A red feather
Is blown into the air by a magician
He wrote a charm on it
For the ladies of the cities of the wind
The words of the stones falling in the wells,
The dances of fire
Are blown into the chamber of the caliph
Becoming sometimes a poem,
Sometimes a virgin pearl
Falling at the feet of Waddah
Who carries it to bed,
A woman crying with desire
Making love with the night and the crazy light of the moon
Raving, singing, ending from where she did not begin,
Regaining
Rediscovering on the bed her virginity,
Ashamed of the night
And the crazy light of the moon
She opens her eyes on the ashes of the fire of a shooting star
Falling on the desert

وريشة حمراء
ينفخها الساحر في الهواء
فتستحيل تارة غزالة
قرونها من ذهب وتارة كاهنة تمارس الغواية
ولعبة النهاية
في حرم الخليفة
وليلِهِ المسكون بالأشباح والملالة

— ٢ —

لم أجد الخلاص في الحب ولكني وجدت الله

— ٣ —

قــبّلتُ مولا تي على سجادة النور وغنيتُ لها موّال
وهبتها شمس بخارى وحقول القمح في العراق
وقمر الأطلس والربيع في أرواد
منحتها عرش سليمان ونار الليل في الصحراء
وذهب الأمواج في البحار
طبعتُ فوق فمها حبي لكل ساحرات العالم ــ النساء ــ
وقبل العشاق
بذرتُ في أحشائها طفلاً من الشعب
ومن سلالة العنقاء

64

And a red feather
Is blown into the air by the magician
Sometimes turning into a gazelle
With horns made of gold
Sometimes into a priestess practicing seduction
And the game of the end
In the harem of the caliph
His night is haunted by ghosts and boredom.

II

I did not find salvation in love, but I found God.

III

I kissed my mistress on the carpet of light
I sang a poem for her
I granted her the sun of Bukhara,
The fields of wheat in Iraq,
The Atlas moon and the spring in Arwad
I granted her the throne of Solomon,
The fire of the night in the desert,
And the gold of the waves in the seas
Upon her lips I printed my love
For all the beautiful women of the world,
And the kisses of the lovers
Within her I sowed
A child from the people
And from the dynasty of the phoenix.

من أين جاءت هذه الأشباح ؟
وأنت في سريرها تنام يا وضاح
لعلها نوافذ القصر ، لعل حرس الأسوار
لم يغلقوا الأ بواب

رأيت في نومي على نهديك نهر الموت
يشق مجراه بلحم الصمت
وكلب صيد ينهش النهدين
وطائر السمان
يـبـدأ في رحيلـه عبر مـدار غـربـة الانسان في العالم والأشياء

ووجه عبد من عبيد القصر
يطل من عيني ومن مرآة هذا الفجر
مقبلاً نهديك في نومي — رأيت العبد
ممدداً وعارياً فوق سرير الورد
مبتسماً للغد

من أين جاءت هذه الأشباح
وأنت في سريرها تنام ياوضاح
لعله الواشي الذي أراح واستراح

IV

Where do these ghosts come from?
While you slept in her bed O Waddah,
Was it the windows of the palace?
Or perhaps the guardians of the walls
Did not close the doors?

V

In my sleep: I saw the river of death on your breast,
Forcing its current in the flesh of the silence
A hunting dog bites your breast
As the quail begin their migration
Following the orbit of human exile in the world and things
A face of a palace slave
Emerges from my eyes and from the mirror of this dawn
In my sleep I saw him kissing your breasts,
Lying naked over the bed of roses
Smiling for the future.

VI

Where are these ghosts from?
While you were sleeping in her bed, O Waddah
Perhaps it was the informer who relieved you

لعله الخليفة
أطلقَ في أعقابك العبد وكلب الصيد والكابوس

— ٧ —

من قبل أن يولد في الكتب
وفي الروايات وفي الأشعار
عطيل كان كائناً موجود
تنهشه عقارب الغيرة يا وضاح
من قبل أن يولد في الكتب
عطيل كان قاتلاً سفاحْ
لكن ديدمونة
في هذه المرة لن تموت
أنت إذن تموت !
أنت إذن تموت !

— ٨ —

عطيل في عمامة الخليفة
يواجه الجمهور
بسيفه المكسور

— ٩ —

لم أجد الخلاص في الحب ولكني وجدت الله

68

Perhaps it was the caliph who sent after you
The slave, the hunting dog, and the nightmare.

VII

Before it came to be in the books,
In the novels and in the poems,
Othello already existed.
The scorpions of jealousy bit him, O Waddah!
Before it came to be in the books
Othello was a bloody killer,
But Desdemona
Will not die this time.
It is you who will die.
It is you.

VIII

Othello in the turban of the caliph
Faces the masses
With his broken sword.

IX

I didn't find salvation in love, but I found God.

متُ على سجادة العشق ولكن لم أمت بالسيف
مت بصندوق وألقيتُ ببئر الليل
مختنقاً مات معي السر ومولا تي على سريرها
تداعب الهرة في براءة، تطرز الأقمار
في بردة الظلام
تروي إلى الخليفة
حكاية عن مدن السحر وعن كنوزها الدفينة
و يدرك الصباح ديدمونة

◻ ◻ ◻

X

I died on the carpet of love,
I didn't die by the sword.
I died inside a box, thrown in the well of night
Suffocated, my secret died with me
And my mistress, on her bed
Innocently caressing the cat, embroidering the moons
In the glacial darkness,
Reciting to the caliph
A tale about cities of magic and their buried treasures
And the morning surprises Desdemona.

* * *

قصــائد حــب
على بوابات العالم السبع

— ١ —

أشردُ من دائرة الضوء إلى الواحات
أهبط من منازل الكواكب الأخرى إلى «اللوفر» مأخوذاً
بسحر العالم المخبوء في اللوحات
بالطائر الأعمى الذي يطارح الغرام
أنثاه في الظلام
بالكلمات و بنار الغسق المطفأة الزرقاء
بوجه «بيكاسو» وراء واجهات الزمن الضائع والغابات
بلمسة الفرشاة
على أديم جسد المرأة والوردة والسماء
بصيحة المهرج السوداء
وهو يرى قناعه يغرق في «اللوار»
أعود للبيت — وفي رأسي ضجيج مدن الأمطار
وعنكبوت النار
أغلق باب غرفتي منتحراً بالغاز

— ٢ —

عرفتُ ، ياحبيبتي ، كل سجون العالم القديم
لكنني أكتشف الآن سجون العالم الجديد

Love Poems at the
Seven Gates of the World

I

I wander from circles of light to the oases
Descending from the houses of other stars
To the Louvre, taken by
The magic of the world hidden in paintings
By the blind bird which makes love
To its mate in the darkness
By the words and the blue embers of the dusk
By Picasso's face behind the windows of lost time and forests
By the touch of the paintbrush
On the body of the woman, the rose, and the sky
By the black cry of the clown
Who sees his mask drowning in the Loire
I return home and in my head
The noise of the cities of rain
And the spider of fire
I shut the door of my room,
Committing suicide with gas.

II

I knew, my love, all the prisons of the old world
I discover now the prisons of the new world

والقهر والاذلال في الأزمنة الحديثة
والموت في أقبية المدينة
وغرف الفنادق اللعينة
عرفتُ : كيف استبدل الطغاة
جلودهم في زمن الهزيمة
ولبسوا أقنعة جديدة
ورددوا الأغنية القديمة
رأيت، ياحبيبتي، كل طغاة العالم القديم
كيف ينامون و يأكلون
كيف يحبون و يضحكون
كيف يموتون و ينتهون
لكنني أكتشف الآن طغاة العالم الجديد
في زمن الطوفان
وثورة الانسان
تبدلتْ أقنعةُ الممثلين، وقع العالم في براثن الملقن
القابع في الظل وتحت رحمة المهرجين : بائعي الأنقاض
فقتلونا قبل أن نحب ، ياحبيبتي ، وصبغوا المسرح بالدماء

— ٣ —

هاجمني اللصوص في باريس
وانتزعوا دفاتري وخضّبوا بالدم
مكعبات النور والأسفلتْ
وتركوني ميتْ

The humiliation and the defeat of our times
The death in the basements of the city
And in the cursed hotel rooms.
I knew: how the tyrants changed
Their skins in times of defeat
And put on new masks
And repeated the same old song
I saw, my love, all the tyrants of the old world
How they slept and ate
How they loved and laughed
How they died and ended
But I now discover the oppressors of the new world
In the time of deluge
And the revolution of man.
The actors changed their masks
The world fell in the clutches of the prompter
Crouching in the shadow,
At the mercy of the clowns: sellers of rubbish.
They killed us before we loved each other
And they dyed the theatre with blood.

III

The thieves assaulted me in Paris
They took my notebook and with blood dyed
The cubes of light and the asphalt
They left me dead

لكنني نهضتُ ، ياحبيبتي ، قبل طلوع الفجر
أحمل زنبق الحقول وعذاب الحرف
للوطن المفتوح مثل القبر

‏— ٤ —

«أركاديا» من بعد «نيسابور»
علقها الساحر في خريطة العالم في دبوس
أحاطها بسور
تفتَّح الجرحُ وسالَ الدمُ فوق كتب السحر وفوق
جسد العاشق والمعشوق

ضاجعها وانتزع الدبوس
وأطفأ الفانوس
فَمن يدقُ البابَ ؟ فالمجوس
عادوا إلى بلادهم تحت ظلال سعف النخيل يبكون
وتبكي الريح

«أركاديا» من بعد «نيسابور»
ما أوحشَ الليل وما أشد بخل النور
في هذه الشوارع الصماء والبيوت
فالحب والحياة والموت على أبوابها ممنوع

‏— ٥ —

قدَّمتُ أوراق انتسابي لرسول الرب
وقوميسار الشعب

But I awoke, oh my love, before dawn
Carrying the lilies of the fields
And the suffering of words
For my nation open like a grave.

IV

After Nishapur
The witch hung Arcadia on the map of the world with a pin
And surrounded it with a wall
The wound opened and blood flowed over the book of magic
And over the lovers' bodies
He made love to her and pulled off the pin
And extinguished the lantern
Who will knock at the doors?
The magi returned to their country
Under the shadows of the palms
Crying with the wind
Arcadia after Nishapur
How the night is desolate, and the light is avaricious
In these deaf streets and houses
Where love, life, and death are forbidden.

V

I presented my application to the messenger of the Lord,
To the deputy of the people

من أجل أن تشرق شمس الله
على الغد المسكون بالخوف و بالأشباح
لكنه سلّمني لغرف التعذيب والسجون والبوليس
والنفي والتشريد
فالعملة الرديئةُ
قد طردت في مدن الأزمنة الحديثةُ
العملة الجيدة الجديدة
وعور «روما» طردوا أشرافها وطردوا الثوار والعشاق
ونصبوا الأحذية المثقوبة
والرمم الصلعاء والأبواق

— ٦ —

من أين يأتي الحب؟ ياحبيبتي ، ونحن محكومون بالاعدام
ونحن في السيرك وفي حديقة الحيوان
واللغة المومس والتاريخ والأوهام
والعقم واليباب
محاصرون منذ ألفي عام
نحاول الخروج من دوائر الأصفار

— ٧ —

أحمل كل ليلة من جبل «القفقاس» هذي النار
أصرخ بالأبواق

For God's sun to rise
On the morrow inhabited by fears and ghosts.
But he handed me over to the rooms of torture,
The prisons and the police,
To exile and banishment.
The old money
Expelled the new money in cities of modern times
The one-eyed men of Rome expelled their nobles,
The revolutionaries and the lovers
And raised up the perforated shoes
And the picked-over bones and the trumpets.

VI

Where does love come from, my love?
If we are condemned to death,
Or in the circus and the zoo?
The language of the prostitute,
History and illusions,
Sterility and waste,
Have encircled us for two thousand years
As we tried to leave the empty circles.

VII

Every night I carry this fire
From the Caucasus Mountains.
I shout in the loud speakers

ومدعي الثورات
في الوطن الغارق في البؤس من المحيط للخليج
والنوم والصلاة :
أسعد حالاً هذه الدواب
وهذه الطبيعة الصامتة الخرساء
من فقراء المدن المرضى
ومن حثالة الأموات في الأرياف
لكنني أصلب عند مطلع الفجر
على الأسوار

□   □   □

At those who proclaim revolution
In this nation,
Drowning in misery,
In sleep and prayers
From the Atlantic Ocean to the Gulf:
These beasts and this silent, mute nature
Are much happier
Than the poor and sick in the cities,
Than the remains of the dead in the countryside
But I am crucified at dawn,
On the walls.

* * *

مجنــون عائشــة

— ١ —

أيقظني في الليل
غناء عصفور، فأوغلتُ مع العصفور
في الغيهب المسحور
لم تستطع سجن الربيع آه في بستانها
رأيت غصناً مزهراً يطل في الديجور
علي من فوق جدار النور
بكيت، فالربيع مرَّ ثم عاد وأنا ما زلت في
بوابة البستان

مُصلياً لغُصنهِ المزهر، للنور الذي يأتي
من الداخل، للألوان
وحاملاً نذري إلى عاصمة الخلافةُ
وحجر الحكمة والخزافة
لعل نجم القطب
يصير لي جسراً على نهر جحيم الحب
فأعبر الصحارى
أمشي وراء ناقتي والفجر قُدامي إلى بخارى
أعود منها حاملاً نذري إلى دمشق
مطارداً وجائعاً للحب
أكتب فوق سورها معلقاتي العشر

82

Aisha's Mad Lover

I

A bird's song
Woke me in the middle of the night
I followed the bird
Deep into the enchanted darkness
She couldn't imprison spring in her orchard
I saw a flowering branch in the gloom,
Leaning over me
From the top of the wall of light
I cried, the spring then returned
And I was still at the gate of the orchard
Praying for its flowering branch,
For the light which comes from inside,
For the colors
Carrying my vows to the capital of the empire
And the stone of wisdom and the legend
Perhaps the polar star
Will become a bridge for me on the infernal river of love
So I can cross the desert
Walking behind my camel, dawn preceding me to Bukhara
I return, carrying my vows to Damascus
Pursued, starved for love
Writing my ten beautiful poems upon its wall

أعقر في بوابة البستان ناقتي وأمضي هائماً في الفجر
ممرغاً وجهي بعطر الزهر
مخبئاً وراء قاسيون
موتي وموت المدن الأخرى التي أصابها الطاعون
وقمر الطفولة المجنون

— ٢ —

خبأتُ وجهي بيدي،
رأيتْ
عائشة تطوف حول الحجر الأسود في أكفانها
وعـنـدمـا نـاديتُـــهـا : هـوت على الأرض رماداً وأنا هويت

فنثرتنا الريح
وكتبت أسماءنا جنباً إلى جنب على لافتة الضريح

— ٣ —

سينتهي النهار
عما قريب، ضمني بين ذراعيك وخُذني نحلةً
عطشى إلى الأزهار

سينتهي النهار
بين ذراعيك و بين البحر والسماء والصحراء
قالت ومدَّت يدها للنار
فاحترقت سفينة في بحر «قزوين»

84

I slaughter my camel at the gate of the orchard
And depart wandering in the dawn
Rubbing my face with the perfume of flowers
Hiding my death behind Qasyun
And the death of other cities stricken by plague
And the demented moon of childhood.

II

I hid my face with my hands
I saw
Aisha in her shroud circling the black stone
And when I called her, she fell to the ground: ashes
I also fell
The wind scattered us
And wrote our names side by side on the tombstone.

III

"Soon
The day will end
Hold me in your arms, take me like a bee
Thirsty for flowers
The day will end
In your arms, in the sea, the sky, the desert,"
She said, as she extended her hand to the fire.
A ship burned in the Caspian Sea

وغاصت في دم الأمواج
وفتحت للبدويِّ وهو في غربته الأبواب
فسار لايلوي على شيء وراء كوكب الصباح والناقة والسراب
فوق سرير هذه الأرض التي تنهار
لتلد الرجال والأفكار

‒ ٤ ‒

وا أسفاهُ ذهبت صيحاتنا سدى

‒ ٥ ‒

تعرّت الأشجار
وسقطت أوراقها وكنستها الريح
ونحن في المنفى: غريبا غربتين، نرتدي الأكفان
نبحث في المعنى عن المعنى وفي سفر الخروج لم نجد بوابة البستان
ولا تعازيم سقوط مطر الأسفار
ولم نجد عشتار
كانت خيام الحب في الصحراء
منهوبة والبدوي حولها يداعب الرباب
وكانت الغزلان
مذعورة تبحث في مصيدة الموت عن الغدران
قالت، وكنا ‒ نبرح «اللوفر» مأخوذين:
غريب غربتين
أنت فخذني نحلة عطشى وضم هذه النحلة في المابين

And sang in the blood of the waves
She opened the gates for the exiled bedouin
He walked dazed behind the morning star,
The camel and the mirage
On the bed of this land which cracks open
To give birth to ideas and men.

IV

Ah! Our cries were in vain!

V

The trees became bare
Their leaves fell and the wind swept them away
We were in exile: two strangers in two exiles
Wearing shrouds
Searching for meaning in the meaning
And in the book of Exodus
We did not find the orchard's gate
Nor the incantations to invoke the rain of voyages
We did not find Ishtar.
In the desert the love tents were stolen
The bedouin was caressing the rebek
The terrified gazelles were searching
For the brooks in the snare of death.
She said, as we were leaving the Louvre, marvelling:
"You are a stranger of two exiles
So take me like a thirsty bee
And hold me in the inbetween world."

بكيت، فالربيع في باريسْ
يُولد مرتين..
في شكل امرأة
ترهص بالبراعم الخضراء والضياء والمطر
تضحك هازئة

— ٦ —

شاة بلا قلبٍ يداوون بها المجنون

— ٧ —

رسائلي وكتبي أحرقها الفاشست
من قبل أن أكتبها في القلب
وختموا فمي بشمع الصمت
لكنني هربت من عاصمة الخلافة
مطارداً وجائعاً للحب
وقاتلا مقتولْ

— ٨ —

في زمن الفوضى وعصر الرعبْ
أشعلت نار الحب

I cried. The spring in Paris
Is born twice
In the form of a woman
Filled with green buds, light, and rain,
Laughing mockingly.

VI

A heartless sheep is used to cure the madman.

VII

The fascists burned
My letters and my books
Before I wrote them in my heart
They sealed my mouth with the wax of silence
But I fled from the capital of the empire,
Pursued, starved for love
Murderer and victim.

VIII

In the times of anarchy and in the era of terror
I lit the fire of love.

وا اسفاه ذهبت صيحاتنا سدى

للغة القبيلة القادمة الجديدة
لوثن القصيدة
أتبع موتي حاملاً رأسي إلى الخليفة
في طبقٍ ، ...
فلتمطر السماء°
دماً وأرجوان

كنا حبيبين : طريدين وملعونَين
ما بين نارين وعالمين
نكابد الغربة في المابين

أواه ماأقسى عذاب الحبْ
حين يغيب في سماء الليل نجم القطب
وحين يعوي الذئب

IX

Ah! Our cries were in vain!

X

For the new language of the upcoming tribe,
For the poem's idol
I follow my death, carrying my head to the caliph
On a plate
Let the sky rain
Purple blood!

XI

We were lovers: pursued and cursed
Between two fires and two worlds
Suffering the exile in the inbetween world.

XII

How harsh is the torture of love
When the polar star disappears in the night sky and
When the wolf howls.

لا أستطيع شرح سر قمر الصحراء
وضحكات الجن في مدافن القبيلة
خواتم تلمع في الظلمة : قالتْ و بكتْ : كم ليلة إليكُ
نظرتُ من كوة قبري وأنا أغالب الأرق
وجسدي يغسله الفجر وخدي فوق خد الأرض
وفمها فوق فمي
لا أحد جاء
ولا ذهبْ
من بحر «قزوين» إلى حلب
أنام في أرجوحة القمر
وسكتتْ ونحن في «اللوفر» ضائعانْ
في زحمة البشر
نسير في أعقابهم أموات
نبحث عن أصواتنا في ضجة الأصوات
نبحث في المعنى عن المعنى، وفي سفر الخروج
لم نجدْ بوابة البستان
ولا تعازيم سقوط مطر الأسفار
ولم نجد عشتار
وكانت الشمس الربيعية

XIII

I can not explain the secret of the desert moon
Nor the laughter of the jinn in the tribal cemetery
Rings shine in the darkness:
She said crying: How many nights
I looked to you from the opening of my grave
Struggling against insomnia
Dawn washed my body
My cheeks on the cheek of the earth,
Her lips on mine
No one came
No one departed
From the Caspian Sea to Aleppo
I sleep in the swing of the moon
She fell silent while we were lost in the Louvre
We were following the steps of the dead crowd
We searched for our voices in the tumult of the voices
For the meaning in the meaning, but in the book of Exodus
We found neither the gate of the orchard
Nor the incantations to invoke the rain of the voyages
We did not find Ishtar.
The spring sun

تصبغ في حمرتها أشجار باريسَ الخزافية
ـ جميلةٌ أنتِ :
وقبّلتُ فم الأرض وقبلت يد الأشجار
ـ جميلةٌ :
وطار عصفورٌ وحط ينقر البذار
فاقتربتْ عائشةُ وداعبته ، فلوى منقاره وطار
أحس بالمطر
من قبل أن يسقط في الشوارع المشمسة المعطار
سنلتقي في الساعة العشرين
قالت ،
وكنت ميتاً داخل نفسي
ضائعاً
مستلباً
طريدْ
مرتحلاً وعائداً وحيدْ
أمشي وراء ناقتي وغصُنها المُزهرُ قدّامي إلى باريس

□   □   □

Colored red the legendary trees of Paris
—You are beautiful
I kissed the mouth of the earth and the hand of the trees
—Beautiful
A bird stopped and picked at the grains
Aisha approached it and caressed it
It twisted its beak and flew away
Feeling the fragrant rain
Before it reached the sunny streets
"We will meet at the twentieth hour,"
She said.
But I was dead within myself,
Lost
Defeated
Pursued
I departed and returned alone
I walked toward Paris behind my camel,
Her branch flowering in front of me.

* * *

كتاب البحر
(١٩٧٣)

The Book of the Sea

(1973)

تحولات نيتو كريس
في كتاب الموتى

— ١ —

أكتب تحت قدم الاميرة ـ العاشقة ـ الكاهنة
المعبودة ـ التمثال ـ أشعاراً، وفوقي
القمر المصري في عباءة النجوم يلتف
وعبر الهرم الكبير يستلقي ـ وفي الحدائق
الوحشية الحمراء محموماً على سجادة النور
أنام ميتاً ـ وجسدي مصر وشعري
النيل ـ محموماً أنام ميتاً وشفتي
فوق فم الأميرة ـ التمثال ـ محموماً وعيني
ترصد السماء في تكوينها وحركات الريح
في الصعيد والنخيل في الواحات والطيور
في وادي الملوك تتبع الكاهنة العذراء
في المدافن السرية المنهوبة الكنوز ـ فوقي
القمر المصري ـ والسمان في هجرته الاولى
إلى منابع الشمس ـ وأنت ترصدين
جسدي. مصر وشعري النيل ـ أنت
وأنا معتنقان ـ عاشقان التقيا من بعد
ألف سنة في التية

Metamorphoses of Netrocres in the Book of the Dead

I

I write poetry at the feet of the adored one /
the lover / the princess / the priestess /
made of marble.
Above me
The Egyptian moon clothed in a gown of stars
Lies across the great pyramid
In the wild red gardens
I feverishly sleep dead
On the carpet of light.
My body Egypt, my hair the Nile.
Feverishly, I sleep dead
My lips upon the lips of the marble princess
My eyes watching the sky in its creation
And the movements of the wind
In the Valley of the Nile.
The palm trees at the oasis, and the birds
In the Valley of the Kings following the virgin priestess
In the secret pillaged tombs.
Above me the rising Egyptian moon
The quail in their first migration
Toward the sources of the sun and you observing
My body Egypt, my hair the Nile.
You and I embraced
Two lovers reunited
After one thousand years of wandering.

– ٢ –

قـدَّمت لها في القداس الأول والثاني والثالث
خبز الجسد ــ الخمر ــ القبلات

– ٣ –

هــا أنــذا عــار عــريَ ســمــاء الــصــيـف
الأ بــدي ــ الــبـحــر ــ الــمــنـفــى ــ الــصــحراء
الكلمات

– ٤ –

أقــوم بـعــد المـوت مــن قـبــرهــا
مــرتــديــاً عـبــاءة الــشــمــس
وزهــرة الــصــبّــار ــ في الــضــوء اذ
تـــذوي أســـى ــ تــاجٌ عـلــى رأسـي
تـعـويــذتــي الأهـــرام في صـمــتـهــا
وسـاحــــرات مـــدن الأمـــس
أتـبـعـهــا مـغــامــراً رائـــيــاً
مـقــتــحــمــاً دائـــرة الـقــوس
وحـامــلاً نــاري وقــيـثـــارتــي
وعـالــم الــضـيــاء والــبـؤس
تـــقــول : أهـــواك . وتـــذوي على

II

In the first, second and third masses
I offered her
The bread made flesh
The wine / the kisses.

III

Here I am
Naked
Like the eternal nudity of the summer sky
The sea / the exile / the desert
The words.

IV

After death I rise from her grave
Wearing the cape of the sun
The thorn flowers / in the grieving light
A crown on my head
My amulet, the pyramids in their silence,
Adventurer, visionary
I follow
The sorcerers of the cities of yesteryear
Invading the circular boundaries
Carrying my fire and my guitar
And the world of light and misery
She says: I love you, and withers

حديقــة الصبّــار في نفـسي
فـراشـة يـصطـادهـا ساحـر
تمـوت بـعـد اللمـس في الـضـوء
مـــرّت على وجــهــي ومـــرّت على
منــازلي حامـلـة مـوتــي
تـاركـة خـيـط دم في الـضـحـى
يـمتـد مـن بـيـت الى بـيـت
أقــول للـسـمــاء في غُـريـهـا
هـل أنـت نـيـتـوكـريـس ؟
هل أنتِ ؟

— ٥ —

زمـن للـحـب أتـى وسـتـأتـي أزمـان للـمـوت

— ٦ —

لـم يـبـق لـنـا إلا الـصـمـت

— ٧ —

تـرحـل الـشـمـس الى الـبـحـر وفي
يـدهـا خـصـلـة شعـر الملـكـةُ
وقـنــاع وثـنــــي ودم
سـال فـوق الـطـرقـات المـهلـكـة

102

Inside the wild, thorny garden within me
A butterfly, chased by a magician
Dying when touched by the light
Landing on my face and
Passing through my houses
Carrying my death, leaving a threat of blood in the morning
From house to house
I say to the sky in its nudity
Are you Netocres?
Is it you?

V

A time for love has come
Times for death will come.

VI

Nothing remains for us except silence.

VII

The sun departs to the sea
In her hand, the queen's tress
A pagan mask and
Blood flowing over the deadly roads.

وأنــا الــكـــاهـــن في مـــعــبـــدهـــا
تـــركـــتـــنـــي فـــوق أرض المـــعـــركـــة
أرتـــدي أقــنـــعـــتـــي مـــنـــتـــحـــراً
قـــاتـــلاً حـــبـــي وحـــب الملـــكـــة

— ٨ —

يختبيء القمر
في شعرها وزنبق السماء
ويحمل الشفق
عبير هذا العالم المغسول بالمطر
وبعد أن ينسدل الستار أبكي وأنا أصغي إلى
العصفور في الأفق يغني — عاشقان التقيا من بعد
ألف سنة في التيه — كنا ها هنا نمارس الحب وكنا —
آه كم أحب عينيك وكم أحب أن أقبل الربيع في
جسمك والحديقة المعطار في شعرك — عبر الهرم
الكبير محموماً أنام ميتاً وجسدي مصر وشعري
النيل — محموماً أنام وأنا أحلم في تدمير هذا العالم
القديم — في إحراق هذا الوثن الصامت — في الفرار
والرحيل من جحيم هذا الأسر نحو مدن الله — وفي
الحلول في الثورة — في نسف جسور الموت — في

I, the priest in her temple
She left me at the battlefield
Wearing my masks, ending my days,
Killing my love and the love of the queen.

VIII

The moon hides
In her hair and in the lilies of the sky
The twilight carries
The perfume of this world washed by rain
When the curtain falls I cry
And I listen to
The birds on the horizon
Celebrating two lovers reunited
After a thousand years of wandering
Here we tasted love
Oh how I love your eyes
How I love to kiss the spring in your body
And the perfumed garden in your hair
Across from the Great Pyramid,
Feverishly, I sleep dead
My body Egypt, my hair the Nile.
Feverishly, I sleep dreaming
Of destroying this ancient world
Of burning this silent idol
Of fleeing this hellish captivity
Towards the cities of God.
I dream of being incarnated in the revolution
Of dynamiting the bridges of death

الرقص على الانقاض ــ في إغراق هذا المركب المليء
بالجرذان ــ في العودة للظهور بعد الموت ــ في
الحضور في العالم ــ في الرحيل للكواكب الاخرى
على ظهر جواد الشعر ــ في البكاء تحت قدم
العاشقة ــ الكاهنة ــ المعبودة ــ التمثال ــ تحت مطر
الخريف والسمان في هجرته الأولى إلى منابع الشمس
وأنت في مهب الريح تبكين وأنت وأنا نعبر بوابات
هذا العالم المكتظ بالجنود والمنتحرين والمجانين
وبالموتى وبالأصفار والمرضى وبالمنتظرين آه كم
أحب عينيك وكم أحب أن أنام في الحدائق
الوحشية الحمراء فوق ذهب النهدين فوق سرة النهر
أنام ميتاً وجسدي مصر وشعري النيل

ــ ٩ ــ

زمن للحب أتى وستأتي أزمان للموت

□ □ □

106

Of dancing in the ruins
Of drowning this boat full of rats
Of reappearing after death
Of complete presence in the world
Of riding the horse of poetry to the other stars
Of crying at the feet of the lover/the priestess /
The adored one / made of marble
Under the autumn rain.
The quail: in their first migration
Toward the sources of the sun
And you sobbing in the wind.
You and I crossing the gates of this world
Crowded with suicidal men, soldiers, insane souls, the dead
And sick people waiting.
Oh how I love your eyes,
How I love to sleep in the red, wild gardens
On golden breasts
Above the river's navel
I sleep dead
My body Egypt, my hair the Nile.

IX

A time for love has come
Times for death will come.

* * *

الأميرة والغجري

‫ـ ١ ـ‬

أدخـل في عـيـنـيـك ــ تخـرجين مـن فـمـي ـ
على جبينك الناصع أستيقظ ــ في دمي تنامين
على سـريـر أمـطـار صـحـاري التتر الحمراء ـ
مجنوناً أناديك بـكـل صـرخـات الـعـالـم
الـوحـشـيـة الـسـوداء واللـغـات ، كـل وجـع
الـعـاشـق في قـاع جـحـيـم المـدن ــ الـعـاشـق
والـولي والـشـهـيـد ــ في دمـي تـنـامـين ــ أنـا
أدخـل في عـيـنـيـك ــ أهـوى ميتاً فـوق سرير
النـار ـــ أستـلـقـي على صـدرك في الحـلـم ـ
تـنـامين على الأهـداب ــ مجـنـوناً أنـاديك ـ
على صـدرك أسـتـلـقـي ـ على صـياح
ديـك الـفـجـر في مملكة الله وفي مملكة السحر
وفي أصقاعها أواصل الرحيلْ

‫ـ ٢ ـ‬

مهاجراً يموتْ
حبي على أسوار هذا اللهب الكـامن في عـيـنـيـك
في صـمـتـك ، في صـوتـك ، في جـبـيـنـك
الممتقع المسحور

108

The Princess and the Gypsy

I

Into your eyes I sink / you leave from my lips / on your clear forehead I awaken / you doze in my blood on the bed of rains from the Tartarian Desert. Crazy I call you in all black, wild cries and in all the languages of the world and in the deep pain of the lover. In the bottom of the cities' hell / the lover / the saint / and the martyr. You sleep in my blood / into your eyes I sink. I fall dead on the bed of fire / I lie on your breast in a dream, you sleep on my eyelashes. Crazy, I call you at the cock's cry. At dawn I lie on your breast in the Kingdom of God and in the kingdom of magic I continue my voyage.

II

My love dies,
Wandering on the walls of the flame
Hidden in your eyes,
In your silence, in your voice,
In your pale enchanted forehead.

حـبــي ، أغـنـيـة كـتـبـتـهـا سـاحـرة فـوق
معابد عشتار
في فجر الانسان الأول ، قبل الألف الثالث من آذار
بعد الطوفان ، وقبل النفي الى الصحراء

من صحراء التتر الحمراء
من باريس إلى صنعاء
كانت عربات الغجر السعداء
تمضي حاملة مولاتي وأنا خلف العربات
عطشي يقتلني ، جوعي ، فأضم غزالة
شمس الواحات
وأضم العالم في كلمات

مجـنـوناً ، كـنـت أنـادي بـاسمـك : كل الأسمـاء
كـل المـعـبودات وكـل زهور الـغـابات وكل الربات
كـل نسـاء العـالم في كتب التاريخ وفي كل اللوحات
كل حبيبات الشعراء
مجنوناً، كنتُ أنادي الله

III

My love, a song written by a sorceress upon
The temples of Ishtar
At the dawn of the first man,
Before March of the third millenium
After the deluge, and before the exodus.

IV

From the red Tartarian Desert
From Paris to Sanaa
The chariots of the happy gypsies were departing
Carrying my queen
And me, behind the chariots
Dying of thirst and hunger.
I embrace the solar gazelle of the oasis
And the world in words.

V

Madly, in your name I called all the names
All the adored women, all the flowers of the forests,
All the goddesses
All the women of the world in the books of history
And in all the paintings
All the lovers of the poets
Madly, I was calling God.

أعـود مـن مملـكـة الله ومـن مملكة السحر على
أجنحة النهـار ــ مجنوناً أناديك بكل صرخات
العـالـم الوحشية السوداء واللغات، كل وجع
الأرض إلى الأمـطـار والـشـمـوس في ليـل شتاء
مـدن الـعـالـم، مجـنـونـاً أنـاديـك ــ وفي
بـيـروت ــ أو ــ بـغـداد ــ أو بـاريـسَ
عـن عـيـنـيـك ــ عـن وجـهـك ــ في قصائد
الـشـعـر وفي واجـهـة المـخـازن الخـضـراء
في شـواطـىء البحار والغابات ــ عن عينيك
عـن وجـهـك في اللـوحـات والـرسـوم ــ
مجنوناً أناديـك ــ على جبـيـنـك الـنـاصع
أسـتـيـقـظ في مـنـتـصف النهار ــ أستلقي
على صـدرك ــ في أصـقـاع عـيـنـيـك ــ
وفي سمائها أواصل الرحيل

VI

I return from the Kingdom of God
And from the kingdom of magic
Carried on the wings of day / madly I call you
In all black cries and in the languages of the world,
In all the suffering of the earth aching for rain and sun
In the wintry night of the cities of the world
Madly I call you / in Beirut, Baghdad or Paris
I search for your eyes / for your face
In poems and in the green store fronts
On the banks of the seas and in the forests
I search for your eyes / for your face
In the portraits and paintings
Madly I call you / on your pure white forehead
I awaken in the middle of the day
I lie on your breasts / in your eyes
And in the blue of their sky
I continue my voyage.

حبي أكبر مني
من هذا العالم
فالعشاق الفقراء
نصبوني ملكاً للرؤيا
وإماماً للغربة والمنفى

باسمك ، مجنوناً ، كنت أنادي الله

□   □   □

VII

My love is bigger than me
Bigger than this world
The poor lovers
Crowned me king of vision,
and imam of banishment and exile.

VIII

Madly
In your name
I was calling God.

* * *

سيدة الأقمار السبعة

‐ ١ ‐

سـيـدة الأقـمـار الـسـبـعـة في داخـلـها ترحل
تـسـتـخـرج يــاقـوت نـهـار الأسـطـورة ‐ تحـلم
بـالـنـجم القطبي ‐ وفي ذاكرة الزمن الموغل
في عـربـات الـغـجـر الـسـاعـين وراء المطـر
الـفـرح ‐ الـنـور ‐ تغـنـي للـيـل الاغـريـقي
وللـنـهـر الـوحشي الـقـادم مـن طـوروسَ
ومـن هـضبـات الـنـوم بـتركستانَ ‐ تغني
سـيـدة الأقـمـار الـسـبـعـة ‐ كـانت ترحل في
داخـلـها ‐ ولنجم قبيلتها فوق البحر الاسود
كـانـت في الحـلـم تصلي ‐ قـالـت : أهواكَ
وقـالـت : رحـل الأغـريـق ، وجـاءت سـفنٌ
غطـت وجه البـحـر ومـدّت لـلأرض جسراً
قـالـت : أهـواك ‐ سـنـرحـل عـن هـذي
الأرض لـبــاريس بـهـذا الـصـيـف الـقـادم
مـن هضبـات النـوم بتركستان ‐ وقالت :
بـدأ المـوت بـهـذا العـالـم يفقد معناهُ ‐ فمي
يـاقوت نهار الأسطورة فوق فم الليل ‐ ونجمُ
الـقـطب على نـافـذة البـحـر يضيء ‐ وأنت

116

The Lady of the Seven Moons

I

The lady of the seven moons travels within herself
Extracting the rubies of the mythic day
She dreams of the polar star
And of the memory of the ancient times in the gypsy chariots
In conquest of the joyful rain / the light
She sings for the Greek night
And for the wild river coming from the Taurus and
From the sleeping hills of Turkestan
The lady of the seven moons travels within herself,
Singing for the star of her tribe on the Black Sea
She prayed in the dream.
She said: I love you
And said: The Greeks departed and ships came
Covering the face of the sea,
Stretching bridges out to the land
She said: I love you
This summer we will leave this country
For Paris
From the sleeping hills of Turkestan
And said: Death began to lose its meaning in this world
My ruby-lipped mouth closed on the lips of the night
The polar star shines on the window of the sea

بعيدٌ عني ـ وأنا في الحلم أراك على أرصفة
المدن البيضاء تسير وحيداً ـ وتموت وحيداً
في الغربة والمنفى ـ قالت: أهواك ـ وقالت ـ
سيدة الأقمار السبعة في داخلها ترحل، لكني
كنت أراها في ضوء نهار العالم، في الشارع
ـ قالت : بدأ الموت بهذا العالم يفقد معناهُ
وأنت بعيد عني وأنا عنك بعيدة

— ٢ —

مملكتي وخرائط أجدادي
تمتد وتمتد
وأنا أنتظر المد

— ٣ —

في «طيبة» ذات البوابات السبع ، العرّافة
قالت : لا تنظر للخلف
الوردة قالت للصيف
وأنا فوق جوادي عبر البحر الأبيض
أتبع صوت العرّافة
للجزر اليونانية

And you far from me
In a dream
I see you on the sidewalk of the white cities,
Walking alone
Dying alone in banishment and exile
She said: I love you.
And said:
The lady of the seven moons
Travels within herself.
But I saw her in the light of the day of the world
In the streets
She said: Death began to lose its meaning in this world
You are far from me
I am far from you.

II

My kingdom and my ancestor's patrimony,
Expanding and expanding
And I am waiting for the rediscovery.

III

At the seven gates of Thebes
The fortune teller said:
Don't look behind you
Like the rose said to the summer,
And I on my horse,
Crossing the White Sea
Following the voice of the fortune teller
To the Greek Islands.

‫ـ ٤ ـ‬

‫«ميلانو» غرقت في البحر‬

‫ـ ٥ ـ‬

‫قـال الـنـهـر الـوحشي القادم من طوروس ومن‬
‫هضبات النوم بتركستان لسيدة الأقمار السبعة:‬
‫يـا قمر الحب، تعالي نهرب عبر جبال الليل‬
‫لـبـاريـسَ ، تـعـالي نـركب أمـواج الـبـحـر ـ‬
‫الاغريق ـ الجزر اليونانية مدت للأرض جسوراً‬
‫رحـل الـبـحـر ومـيـلانـو ظـهـرت مـن بين‬
‫الأشـرعـة الـبـيـض ـ تـعـالي نـهـرب‬
‫عـبـر جبـال الليل ـ تعالي ـ قالت : أهواك‬
‫ومـدّت يدهـا للـقـمـر المصلوب على بـوابة‬
‫بيـت الزوج النـائم كـالدب القطبي على‬
‫أطـراف الـصـحـراء ـ وقالت : بدأ الموت بهذا‬
‫العـالم يـفقد معناه ـ ومـدّت يدها الأخرى‬
‫نـحوي ـ سقط الـنـيـزك في الـغـابة ، أحرقَ‬
‫كل الأشجار ـ الجزر اليونانية تغرق في دمعي‬
‫هـيـلين تـغـنـي فـوق الأولمـب ـ تـعـالي ـ‬
‫ركـضـت نـحـوي، والـتـقـت الأيـدي ـ‬
‫ووقـفـنـا تحت الأسوار ـ المدن الطينيةُ تبكي‬

IV

Milan drowned in the sea.

V

The wild river coming from the Taurus
And from the sleeping hills of Turkestan
Said to the lady of the seven moons:
O moon of love, let us flee to Paris
Over the mountains of night
Let's ride the waves of the Aegean Sea
The Greek Islands were bridges to the land
The sea departed and Milan appeared
From among the white sails
Let's run away over the mountains of night:
Come, she said: I love you
She extended her hand to the moon,
Crucified on the gates of the sleeping husband,
Like a polar bear on the edges of the desert
And said: Death began to lose its meaning in this world.
She extended her other hand towards me
The shooting star fell in the forest, burning all the trees
The Greek Isles drowned in my tears
Helen singing over Mount Olympia: Come!
She ran towards me
Our hands joined
We stopped at the walls,
The clay cities crying and

والصيف الهندّي الأحمر فوق جواد الشمس السوداء ــ وأنت بعيدٌ عني وأنا عنكَ بعيدة

— ٦ —

العرّاف الأعمى
يقرأ في مرآة البحر الأبيض
طالع مولاتي
سيدة الأقمار السبعة

□   □   □

The red Indian summer holding itself
Over the horse of the black sun
You are far from me
I am far from you.

VI

In the mirror of the White Sea
The blind fortune teller
Reads
The fortune
Of her highness, my queen
The lady of the seven moons.

* * *

العاشقة

‫- ١ -‬

كانت تصغي بجوارحها و بعينيها للموسيقى الوثنية
للنهر المتنهد في غابات جبال الأطلس ،
للمدن الأسطورية ،
للساعات الضائعة الجوفاء
لثمار الليل الذهبية فوق سرير الأمطار
كانت في أحضان الزوج النائم عذراء
تلعب بالقمر الحافي فوق رؤوس الأشجار
تتبع موت فراشات ربيع مات على طاولة المقهى
وتمد يديها ضارعة
فالموعد فات
والليل على شرفات البحر الأبيض يسترخي
محموم النظرات

‫- ٢ -‬

بـيـروت اغـتـصـبـت في هـذي الليـلـة في الحـانـات

The Lover

I

With her eyes
And all her soul
She was listening to pagan music,
To the sighing river in the forests of the Atlas Mountains,
To the legendary cities,
To the empty, lost hours,
To the golden fruits of the night above the bed of rain
In the arms of the sleeping husband
She was a virgin,
Playing with the barefoot moon above the treetops
Following the death of butterflies of a dead spring
Upon the cafe tables
She implored with her hands
The hour of the rendezvous passed
The night with feverish eyes was descending
On the balconies of the White Sea.

II

On this night Beirut was raped in the taverns.

كانت تصغي، لكن العاشق مات
في المقهى منتظراً: سيدة الأقمار السبعة
في موسيقى «باخ»
وقصائد «أيلوار»
في الأسبوع الرابع من كانون الأول، في أعياد الميلاد
كانت تتمنى : لو مات العالم
لو زحفت كالكلبة تحت الأمطار
لو ضربت بسياط من نار
لو حُملت قرباناً للبحر المستلقي
تحت الشرفات

لكن الموعد فات

كانت تفصلها عني :
سنوات من سفرٍ ــ أجيال
أنهارٌ ــ قارات
كتبٌ ــ مدن ــ أسوار
لكني كنت أراقبها من ثقب الباب

□ □ □

III

She was listening, but the lover died
In the cafe, waiting for the lady of the seven moons
In the music of Bach
And in the poems of Eluard
In the fourth week of December
At Christmas
She was wishing that the world had died,
That she had crawled like a bitch under the rain,
That she had been stricken by the whips of fire,
That she had been carried as sacrifice to the outstretched sea
Under the balconies
But the hour of the rendezvous had passed.

IV

Separating her from me:
Years of travels / generations,
Rivers / continents,
Books / cities / walls.
But I was always watching her
From the crack in the door.

* * *

سيرة ذاتية لسارق النار
(١٩٧٤)

- المخاض
- قصائد عن الفراق والموت
- الزلزال
- السمفونية الحجرية

Autobiography of the Thief of Fire

(1974)

- *Labor Pains*
- *Poems on Separation and Death*
- *The Earthquake*
- *The Gypsy Symphony*

المخـاض

ــ ١ ــ

قالَ: اقتليني، فأنا أحبُ عينيكِ
ومن أجلك أبكي
كانت الكنائس القوطية الحمراء في بطاقة البريد
تستحم بالشمس
و بيكاسو غلاف العدد الأخير من مجلة «الحياة»
يرنو لضياء العالم الأخير
قالت: لغةُ الوردةِ في حدائق الليلِ
على شفاهنا تزهرُ
مـن يـبـكي على أسوار هـذي المـدن ــ الملاجـىء ــ القبور؟
منْ يبكي على شطآن بحر الروم في منتصف الليل؟
ومن يفك لغز الوحش في «طيبةَ»؟
فالعالم في العصر الجليدي على أبوابه الجنود
والطغاةُ ، يحجبون بالجرائد الصفراء : نارَ الليلِ
والنبيذ والقيثار
قالت: بحضور غائب مسكونة ، أتبعُ
موت قمر الثلج على نافذة المدينة ــ الاسطورة
الجميع كانوا يكذبونَ
وأنا بوحدتي مملوءة ، أسقط إعياء على
طاولة المقهى
ونارُ الليل في كأس النبيذ تشعل البحر

Labor Pains

I

He said: Kill me. I love your eyes
And for you I cry.
The red gothic churches on the postcards were
Bathing in the sun
And Picasso, on the cover of the last issue of Life Magazine
Was looking at the final light of the world.
She said: The language of the rose in the gardens of night
Blossoms on our lips.
Who cries upon the walls of these cities / shelters / graves?
Who cries at the shores of the Roman Sea at midnight?
And who solves the mystery of the Beast of Thebes?
The soldiers and the tyrants stand
At the gates of the ice age world
Hiding the flame of the night, the wine, the guitar
With yellow newspapers.
Haunted by an absent presence, she said:
I follow the death of the snow moon
At the window of the city / the myth.
All were lying,
And I, filled with my loneliness,
Fall ill at the cafe table,
The flame of the night in the wine cup
Ignites the sea.

أراك قادماً من آخر الدنيا ، على شفاهنا
تُزهرُ بعضُ الكلمات
ينتهي عذابُنا
لنبدأ الرحلةَ من جديد

— ٢ —

مـن قبـل أن تـولد في ذاكـرة البـحر وفي ذاكـرة الوردة والعصفور
ماتت على نوافذ الفجر وفي دفاتر الوحشة : نيسابور
تاركة حضورهـا الغـائـب في حدائق الليل وفي أجنة الزهور
وخصلة من شعرها فوق سرير المطر المهجورْ

— ٣ —

قال : اقتليني ، فأنا أحب عينيكِ
وضاع الصوتْ

— ٤ —

شوارع المدينةُ
موحشةٌ ، بعدكِ ، حتى الموتْ

132

I see you coming from the end of the world
On our lips some words blossom
Our suffering ends
So we start the voyage again.

II

Before it was born in the memory of the rose and the bird
Nishapur died on the desolate notes
And upon the windows of dawn,
Leaving its absent presence in the gardens of the night
And in the seeds of the flowers
And a braid of her hair upon the abandoned bed of rain.

III

He said: "Kill me. I love your eyes."
The voice was lost.

IV

The streets of the city were
Desolate without you until death.

كان مذيعُ نشرة الأخبار في منتصف الليلِ

يُعيدُ الموجزَ . الأطفالُ كانوا

نائمينَ . كانتْ

السماءُ حبلى ، شارة غامضة ،

صيحةُ انسان يموتُ في مكان ما . رأيتُ البرق

في حربته : يشق جوفَ الليل

والمستنقع الجاثم في أحشائهِ

رأيتُ : نيسابور في سريرها عارية تضاجع التنين

كان وجهها الميت في حنوطه مبللاً بعرق الليل

وبالحمى ، رأيتُ : بطنها منتفخاً

ويدها تحتضن التنين، تمتد جذوراً في عروق الأرضِ

كانت في سرير المطر ــ الوجود تلتف، تنامُ

ومذيع نشرة الأخبار في منتصف الليل

يعيد الموجز. انتظرتُ : أن تستيقظي أيتها

الكاهنةُ ــ العذراءُ . فالعالمُ في العصر الجليديِّ

على أبوابه الجنودُ والطغاةُ

يحجبون بالجرائد الصفراء : نارَ الليلِ

والنبيذ والقيثار ، لكنكِ

أوصدت بوجهي البابَ والتابوت

أغلقت عيونَ الفجر

أرسلتِ ورائي العسَسَ ــ اللصوصَ

أرسلتِ كلابَ الصيد ، ناديتُك ، ضاعَ

الصوتُ في الهواء : كانوا يكذبون كلما داهمهم

صقيعُ هذا الليل ، كانوا يكذبون ، انهم

The newscaster at midnight was
Repeating the news summary.
The children were sleeping.
The sky was full, a vague signal,
A cry of a man dying somewhere.
I saw: the lightning bolt
Breaking the heart of the night
And the crouching swamp within him.
I saw: Nishapur in her bed naked,
Making love to the dragon
Her dead face was embalmed, wet with the sweat of night
And with fever.
I saw: her swollen belly
And her hand, embracing the dragon,
Stretching like roots in the earth
She was in the bed of the rain / the existence
Curled up, asleep,
And the newscaster at midnight
Repeated the news summary. I waited:
For you to wake up
O you priestess / virgin
At the gates of the ice age world
The soldiers and tyrants hide
The flame of the night, the wine, and the guitar
With their yellow newspapers.
But you closed the door and the casket in my face
You shut the eyes of dawn
You sent the thieves and the hunting dogs after me
I called you but the sound disappeared in the air:
They were all lying whenever the frost of this night
Fell upon them
They were lying, O my lady,

سيدتي ، كلابُ صيدِ الملكِ ــ الأمير . كانوا
يكتبون الشعر عن عينيك والثورة من خلف
متاريس الأمير ــ الورق العتيق ، من خلف
متاريس سفارات ملوك البدو والبترول .
كانوا يكذبون، انهم ، سيدتي،
أحذيةٌ جديدة معروضة للبيع في أسواق «بيروت»
وفي أسواق هذا الوطن الممتدِ
كالجرح من المحيط للخليج . قالتْ : لغةُ الوردةِ
في حدائق الليل على شفاهنا تزهرُ
من يبكي على أسوار هذي المدن ــ الملاجىء ــ القبور ؟

من يبكي على شطآن بحر الروم في منتصف الليلِ
أراهُ قادماً من آخر الدنيا
على شفافه تزهرُ بعضُ الكلمات
ينتهي عذابهُ
ليبدأ الرحلةَ من جديدْ

□   □   □

136

Those hunting dogs of the king / prince
Were writing poetry about your eyes, about the revolution
From behind the barricades of the prince / ancient paper
From behind the barricades of the embassies
Of the bedouin and oil kings.
They were lying, O my lady
They are in new shoes,
Marked for sale in the markets of Beirut
And in the markets of this nation,
Lying like a wound from the Ocean to the Gulf
She said: The language of the rose in the garden of the night
Blossoms on our lips.
Who cries upon the walls of these cities / shelters / graves?
Who cries upon the shores of the Roman Sea at midnight?
I see him coming from the end of the world
On his lips some words blossom
His suffering ends
To begin his voyage again.

* * *

قصائد عن الفراق والموت

‐ ١ ‐

قمرٌ عراقي على الأشجار يمسح خده
و يدق باباً بعد باب دون جدوى
فالأميرة قبل ان يستيقظ الفقراءُ، كانتْ
في جناح يمامة رحلتْ
ولم تقُل : الوداع ! فمنْ رآها
فَلْيُبلغها السلامْ

‐ ٢ ‐

كان أمير القمرْ
فوق جواد النار في سهوب أسبانيا
التي تزحف نحو البحرْ
يحمل في خاتمه أولاده السبعةَ، لمّا مر في
جنينةٍ مسكونةٍ بالسحرْ
فكمنتْ صبيةٌ له ، ونادت نجله الأصغرَ
أغوته بتعويذةِ حبٍ ، عقلت لسانهُ وطلسمتْ
عيُونه بالسر
وعندما همَّ بها
همّت به : اختفى

138

Poems on Separation and Death

I

An Iraqi moon wipes its cheeks on the trees
Knocking at door after door in vain.
Before the poor woke up, the princess
Had departed on a dove's wing
Without saying farewell
May whoever sees her
Salute her.

II

The prince of the moon was
Riding the fire horse
On the plains of Spain
Which crawled to the sea,
Carrying his seven sons in his ring.
When he passed through an enchanted garden
A young woman lay in wait for him
Calling his youngest son.
She seduced him with a love spell
Which rendered him mute and
Sealed his eyes with secrets
When he took her,
She took him: he disappeared.

وضاع الولدُ الأصغرُ
في سهـوب أسبانيا التي تزحف نحو البحر
ومنذ ذاك الزمن البعيد، والأمير
يصيح في الليل، ينادي نجله الأصغر، والسهوبُ لاتجيبْ

— ٣ —

أكلما مررتُ بالقنطرةْ
أراكِ : ياسيدة النساء
تغتسلين، وجمالُ وجهكِ الفتان
تمضي به المياه
فلا تظني : عندما أغني
بأنني فرحانْ
فانني أموت كالعصفورْ
إن لم أغن لكِ ، ياسيدةَ النساء

— ٤ —

أشجارُ ورد غرسوها فوق قبر شاعر مجهولْ
كانت الى جوارها تأوي العصافيرُ
وتبكي امرأة مجهولة طوال يوم السبتْ
وعندما جف ترابُ القبرْ
اختفى قناع المرأة المجهولة ، الأوراد ماتتْ
والعصافير، وظل القبر
تحوم فوق صمته سحابةٌ مسحورة طوال يوم السبتْ

140

The young son was lost
On the plains of Spain
Which crawled into the sea.
Since that ancient time
The prince cries at night, calling his youngest son
But the plains do not reply.

III

Every time I cross the bridge
I see you bathing, O mistress of women,
The beauty of your fascinating face
Drifting with the current.
So do not think
That I rejoice when I sing
I die like the bird
If I don't sing to you
O mistress of women.

IV

They planted roses on the grave of an unknown poet
The birds sought refuge there
An unknown woman cried all Saturday
When the earth on the grave dried up
The mask of the unknown woman disappeared
The roses wilted
The birds died.
All Saturday
An enchanted cloud hovered
Over the silence of the grave.

قال : انتظريني عند البوابات السبعْ
سنوات سبعٌ مرتْ
كبرتْ أشجارُ الغابة فيها
جفَّ النبعْ
والمرأة لم تفِ بالوعدْ
لكن العاشقْ
ظل طوال السنوات السبعْ
يذهب كل مساء ، منتظراً ، عند البوابات السبع

□   □   □

V

He said: Wait for me at the seven gates
Seven years passed
The trees in the forest grew
The spring dried up
And the woman did not keep her promise.
But for seven years
The lover waited every evening
At the seven gates.

* * *

الزلـــزال

تُشرق شمسُ الله في عينيك اذ تغربُ في قوارب

الصيد على شواطىء المغرب

حيث فقراء الأطلس المنتظرون معجزات القمر الوليّ

في الأضرحة ــ الطلاسم ــ الذبائح ــ النذور، حيثُ

النسوةُ المكفنات بسواد الخرق ــ الأطمار

حيث الشاعرُ الأندلسي يرتدي عباءة الريح

يطير حاملاً قيثاره فوق جبال النوم

فوق المدن المفتوحة، المقطوعة الأثداء ، حيثُ

القمر الولي في عيون قارعي طبول الملك الأخيرِ

في «قرطبة» يغيب في البحر ،

أراك : تدخلين ملجأ الأيتام

تحملين عصفوراً ووردتين من حدائق «الحمراء»

تبكين على سريرك البارد في منتصف الليلِ

وفي الصباح من شرفة «افريقيا»

تُطلين على عُريك من زاوية المقهى

أراكِ ــ وأنا أحمل من منفى الى منفى

تراب الـوطن ــ القصائد الممنوعة ــ الجرائد السرية ــ النار ؟

The Earthquake

I

God's sun shines in your eyes when setting on the
Fishing boats at the Moroccan shores
Where the poor of the Atlas await the miracles
Of the moon saint
At the tombs / the magic charms / the sacrifices /
The solemn vows.
Where women are shrouded in ancient tattered blackness,
And the Andalusian poet wears the cape of the wind
Carrying his guitar, flying over the sleeping mountains,
Over the open, breastless cities
Where, in the eyes of the last king of Cordoba's drummers,
The moon saint disappears in the sea.
I see you: entering the orphanage
Carrying a bird and two roses from the gardens of Alhambra,
Crying on your cold bed in the middle of the night
And in the morning from the window of Africa
Overlooking your nudity from the corner of the cafe.
I see you: while from exile to exile
I carry the soil of the nation /
The forbidden poems / the secret newspapers / the fire.

أراك : تعبرين السوق والبوليسُ في المحضر

في مخافر الحدود محموماً يغطي بالدبابيس و بالشمع

وجـوه فقـراء الأطـلـس ــ الخـرائـط ــ الـذبـائـح ــ الأضـرحة ــ النذور

حيث الشاعرُ الأندلسي في سجون العالم الجديدِ

في زنزانةِ الخليفةِ الاخيرِ في «قرطبة» يموتْ

— ٢ —

توقفت عائشة ، فالباص لايذهبُ في الليلِ

الى كوبا ، ولايعودْ

— ٣ —

كـلُ الـدروبِ أصبحتْ بعيدة، لكنها مشمسةٌ تلوحُ من بعيدْ

— ٤ —

قالَ : أعودُ ــ غارسيا لوركا ــ اذا ما انتصف الليلُ

وفي الوادي الكبيرنامتْ الزهورْ

— ٥ —

العاشقُ الأندلسي عصبوا عيونهُ وقَتلوهُ

قبل أن ينتصف الليلُ وقبل أن يصيحَ الديكْ

I see you: crossing the market and
The police, in their report, at the border stations
Feverishly cover with pins and wax the faces of the Atlas poor /
The maps / the sacrifices / the tombs / the solemn vows.
The Andalusian poet in the prisons of the new world
Is dying in the prison cell of the last caliph of Cordoba.

II

Aisha stopped.
The bus doesn't go to Cuba at night,
Nor does it return.

III

All the roads are distant but look sunny from afar.

IV

He said: I will return Garcia Lorca
At midnight
And in the big valley, the flowers slept.

V

The Andalusian lover: blindfolded and killed
Before midnight and before the cock's cry.

قالت : رأيتُ الملكَ الأخيرَ في «قرطبة» كانَ
بسيف الخشب المكسور فوق عرشه متكئاً
مكتئباً ، يهتز مثل ريشةٍ في الريح ،
كان حوله السياف والشاعر والمنجم المخصيُ
في بلورة محدقاً، يقول : مولايَ
أرى سحابةً حمراء فوق هذه المدينةِ المفتوحةِ
المقطوعة الأثداء ، مولاي أرى نسراً عظيماً
جاثماً فوقك ــ مولايَ أرى الحريقَ في كل مكانٍ
وجواري القصر والغلمان بالسم يموتون ، أراك
عارياً أعمى على قارعة الطريق في «قرطبة» تشحذُ
قالت : عندها أومأ للسياف أن يقطعَ
رأسَ الشاعر ــ النديم .
مرت ليلةٌ
وفي الصباح أُحـــرق المنجمُ المخصي بالتنور
«مولايَ» انتهت
فالباصُ لايذهبُ في الليل الى كوبا ولايعودُ ،
والجرائد الصفراء لاتحجب وجه فقراء الأطلسِ
المنتظرين معجزات القمر الولي
قالت ، وبكتْ : في ملجأ الايتام
كنا نخدع البوليس في منتصف الليل
ونمضي حاملين الصحف السريةَ ــ القصائدَ الممنوعةَ ــ النار

148

VI

She said: I saw the last king of Cordoba
Leaning over his throne with his broken wooden sword,
Depressed, shaking like a feather in the wind.
Around him the executioner, the poet
And the castrated fortune teller
Staring into the crystal,
Saying: My lord,
I see a red cloud over this open, breastless city
My lord, I see a great eagle sitting on you,
My lord, I see fire everywhere,
The palace slaves poisoned to death
I see you blind and naked at the open road in Cordoba, begging.
She said: At this time the king motioned to
The executioner to chop off
The head of the poet — companion.
A night passed
In the morning the castrated fortune teller
Was burned in the oven.
The word: "My lord," is dead.
At night, the bus does not go to Cuba
Nor does it return
The yellow newspapers do not conceal the faces
Of the Atlas poor,
Waiting for the miracles of the moon saint.
She said, and cried: in the orphanage
We deceived the police at midnight
We carried the secret newspapers / the forbidden poems /
The fire

الى الأضرحة ــ الطلاسم ــ الذبائح ــ النذور
حيث النسوةُ المكفناتُ بسواد الخِرق ــ الاطمار
حيث الشاعرُ الاندلسي يرتدي عباءة الريح
و يبكي حبه الضائع في «قرطبة»
رأيت عصفوراً ووردتين مـن حـدائق «الحمراء» في شَعرِكِ
كان «اللعبي» يعبر الشارع :
من منفى الى سجن ومن سجن الى منفى
تقولين ، أنا أقول أيضاً : « إنه الزلزالُ »
في «الأطلس» في كوبا رقصنا
عندما أمطرت السماء
قال ضاحكاً «ألبرتُ» : من أين يجيء النومُ
والبحر وليٌّ عاشقٌ
يحمل في سلته المحارَ والأسماكَ واللؤلؤ
هل عاد من الغابات « جيفارا » ؟
رقصنا عندما أمطرت السماء والبحر ولــيٌّ كان
يبكي حبهُ الضائع في المغرِب . قالتْ وتقولينَ
أنا أقولُ أيضاً :
إنه الخليفةُ الأخيرُ في « قرطبة » يموتْ

□   □   □

150

To the tombs / the magic charms / the sacrifices /
The solemn vows
Where the women are shrouded in ancient tattered blackness
And the Andalusian poet wears the cape of the wind,
Crying for his lost love in Cordoba.
I saw a bird and two roses in your hair
From the garden of Alhambra
La`bi was crossing the street:
From exile to prison and from prison to exile
You said, and I say too:
It is the earthquake.
We danced in the Atlas and in Cuba
When the sky rained.
Alberti asked laughingly: where does sleep come from?
And the sea is a saint and a lover
Carrying seashells, fish, and pearls in a basket
Has Guevara returned from the forests?
We danced when the sky rained.
And the sea was a saint,
Weeping for its lost love in Morocco.
She said, you say, and I say too:
The last caliph in Cordoba is dying.

* * *

السمفونية الغجرية

كان المغني الغجريُّ يرشقُ العذراء بالوردةِ ،
والعذراء مثلَ ريشةٍ تدور حول نفسها ،
تحاول اللحاق بالليل الذي كان على مَشارف «الحمراء»
مقتولاً تغطي صدره الخناجرُ ــ الزنابقُ ــ النجومُ .
كان الغجريُّ شاحباً يطرد في غنائه الأشباحَ
كانت يدهُ ترسم في الهواء شارةَ الغريق ــ العاشق ــ المخدوع
والعذراء مُثل ريشةٍ تطيرُ خلف يده الواجفة ، الضارعة
« الحمراء » كان غارقاً كعهده بالصمت .
صاحَ الغجريُّ : استيقظي أيتها الأعمدةُ ــ الهياكل ــ الأقواسُ
يامكعبات النور في قصيدة المستقبل ــ النبوءة ــ الرحيلِ
صاح : استيقظي أيتها الأسطورةُ ــ القبيلةُ ــ
العذراء مدت يدها ليده وعانقتها ،
رقصا معاً وأصبحا لسانَ لهبٍ
فاشتعلت في شَعرها الوردةُ
صاح الغجريُّ : احترقي أيتها الصغيرةُ الحسناءُ .
مال رأسها ، تلاقت العيون والشفاهُ
هذا زمنُ الموت على وسادة الربيع
مال رأسه ، فاحتضنته وهوييكي
يطرد الأشباح في غنائه الصاعدِ من قرارة

The Gypsy Symphony

I

The gypsy singer was striking the virgin with the rose,
And the virgin, like a feather, was twirling around herself,
Trying to seize the slaughtered night,
Its chest covered with daggers / lilies / stars
At the borders of Alhambra.
The pale gypsy exorcised the ghosts with his singing
In the air his hand drew the sign of the
Drowned/lover/deceived. The virgin, like a feather, was flying
Behind his imploring, tremulous hand.
Alhambra was drowning as usual in silence
The gypsy cried: Wake up you pillars / temples / arches
O prisms of light in the poem of the future /
The prophecy / the voyage!
He cried: Wake up you myth / tribe!
The virgin stretched her hand towards his and clasped it
They danced together and became a flame
The rose blazed in her hair.
The gypsy cried: Burn, you beautiful little one!
She tilted her head, their eyes and lips met
This is the time of death on spring's pillow.
He tilted his head, she held him close to her as he cried,
Exorcising the ghosts with his singing,

الاسطورة ــ القبيلةِ

«الحمراء» كان غارقاً كعهده بالصمت ، والفجرُ

على أبوابه يرسم أشجاراً وقبرات ليلٍ راحلٍ .

تلاقت العيونُ والشفاهُ

صاح الغجريُّ خائفاً : توقفي أيتها الريشة في

مدار هذي اللعبة ــ الفاجعة .

العذراء دارت دورتين

وقفتْ ،

تحـاولُ اللحـاقَ بالليل الذي كـان على مشـارف «الحمراء»

مقتولاً تغطي صدرهُ الخناجرُ ــ الزنابق ــ النجومْ

— ٢ —

توقفتْ هجرةُ أحزان المغني

وقعَ الطائر في الكمين ،

مرت عربـاتُ الغجر ، الليلة ، في وحول هذا

الشارع المحاصر ، المسكون بالأشباح .

كان الغجريُّ يمسح السكين بالمنديل ثم

يعبر الشارع محشوراً مع الأشباح في المقهى

يغني خائفاً لنفسه . قارئةُ الكف له قالتْ

هناك مدن رائعة أخرى وراء النهر، حيثُ الشمسُ

لا تغيب في الليل ، ولايخدعُ فيها العاشق ــ الغريقُ

في منتصف النهر، ولا ترحل فيها الريشةُ ــ العذراءُ

صاح اقتربي : فانني رأيتُ عينيكِ بأسفارِ

النجوم ــ الريح ،

Rising from the depths of the myth / tribe.
Alhambra was drowning as usual in silence
At its gates, the dawn was drawing trees,
And larks of a passing night.
Their lips and their eyes met
The gypsy cried in fear: Stop, you feather
In the circle of this tragic game.
The virgin turned twice,
Stopped,
Trying to seize the slaughtered night,
Its chest covered with daggers / lilies / stars
At the border of Alhambra.

II

The flight of the gypsy's sadness stopped
The bird fell in the trap
Tonight, the chariots of the gypsies
Passed in the mud of this road besieged by ghosts.
The gypsy wiped his knife with a handkerchief,
Then he crossed the street,
Sliding himself between the ghosts in the cafe,
Singing in fear for himself.
The palm reader said to him:
There are other marvelous cities beyond the river
Where the sun does not set
And where the drowned / lover is not deceived
In the middle of the river
And where the virgin / feather does not go.
He cried: Come close! I saw your eyes in
The books of the stars / the wind.

أجدادي على بوابة الشمس
وفي المدافن السرية ــ الكهوف، كانوا يرسمونَ
وجهك الغارقَ بالنور
وكانوا، كلما عاد الربيعُ احتفلوا بعودةِ الروح
الى الطبيعة الميتة .
الأشباح غابتْ واختفى المقهى
وكان الغجريُّ راكعاً يبكي ،
وكانت يدهُ في يدها
قارئةُ الكف، له قالتْ : هناك مدن رائعةٌ أخرى
وراء النهر ، فارحلْ
فهُنا ، الخطوط في كفكَ ، لا تقولُ شيئاً
طفقت تبكي ،
وكان الغجريُّ راكعاً يبكي على مكعبات النور
في قصيدة المستقبل ــ النبوءة ــ الرحيل
صاح آستيقظي أيتها الاعمدةُ ــ الاقواسُ
في وحول هذا الشارع المحاصر، المسكون بالأشباح
كانت يدهُ في يدها صماء ، لا تقولُ شيئاً
نهضت قارئةُ الكف ودارتْ دورتين ،
وقفتْ ،
تحاول اللحاق بالليل الذي كان على مشارف «الحمراء»
مقتولاً تغطي صدره الزنابق ــ الخناجر ــ النجومْ

□   □   □

156

My ancestors at the gate of the sun
And in the secret tombs / caves,
Were painting your face,
Drowned in light
And upon the return of spring
They celebrated the return of the soul
To the inanimate nature.
The ghosts scattered, the cafe disappeared
The gypsy was on his knees crying
His hands in hers.
The palm reader said to him:
There are magnificent cities out there,
Beyond the river
So, depart
Here, the lines in your palm are mute.
She began to cry
The gypsy was on his knees crying on the prisms of light
In the poem of the future / the prophecy / the voyages.
He cried: Wake up you pillars / arches!
In the mud of this street haunted by ghosts
His hand was in her hand, deaf-mute.
The palm reader stood and turned twice,
Stopped,
Trying to seize the slaughtered night,
Its chest covered with daggers / lilies / stars
At the borders of Alhambra.

* * *

قمر شيراز
(١٩٧٥)

Shiraz's Moon

(1975)

الى رفائيل ألبرتي

– ١ –

آخر طفل في المنفى ، يبكي «مدريد»

يغني نار الشعراء الأسبان المنفيين الموتى : لوركا

ـ ماشادو ،

آخر عملاق في معطفه يبكي

تحت النجم القطبي

وتحت الثلج

وقفنا بجوار عمود النور . وكانت «روما تبحث عن روما»

ناديتك : ألبرتي !

فأجاب الشعرُ

أضاء : البرق الكامن في سحب كانت تمضي نازفة

في ليل المنفى :

كلَ عذابات الأسبان

أجابت : روما

وأجابت : موسيقى البحر الوحشية . كنا أطفالاً

أوغلنا في الغابة ، لكن الموسيقى هدأت والبحرُ

توارى في كتب كانت تحكي عن نور يأتي من

داخل «توليدو» . عن نجم عربي يتجول في

أوربا و ينام على بوابة «توليدو» كنا أطفالاً

For Rafael Alberti

I

The last child in exile cries for Madrid,
Celebrates the flame of the dead, exiled
Spanish poets: Lorca,
Machado
The last giant cries under his coat,
Under the polar star,
Under the snow
We stood next to the column of light
"Rome was searching for Rome"
I called you: Alberti!
Your poetry answered me
The hidden lightning inside the bleeding clouds
Passing in the night of exile
Illuminated all the suffering of the Spanish people.
Rome answered me
As did the wild music of the sea. We were children,
We penetrated the forest, but the music
Subsided, and the sea
Disappeared into books which spoke about a light
Coming from the heart of Toledo,
About an Arabian star travelling in Europe,
Sleeping at the gates of Toledo.
We were children

في الوطن ــ المنفى ، نبني مدناً للحب . أجاب :
الشعر ــ البرق ــ الموسيقى
آخر عملاق في معطفه يبكي ، ويجف المطرُ
الأسباني على أشجار الغابة «ماشادو»
في الفجر يموت مريضاً ووحيداً . كل عذاباتِ
الأسبان تعود ، لتولد منها : هذي النار
الزرقاء : الكتب ــ الموسيقى ــ الأشعار ــ
اللوحاتُ
وقفنا . ناديتك : ألبرتي !
فأجاب : الطفل ــ الرجل ــ الشعر
وكانت روما تبحث عن روما في منشور سري
أو عين امرأة تسبر أغوار سماء لم تمطر،
أو كأس نبيذ لم يُشرب. كانت روما تنهض
من تحت الأنقاض
وقفنا تحت عمود النور، رأينا : نار الشعراء
الأسبان المنفيين الموتى : لوركا ــ ماشادو
ورأينا : العربي القادم من «توليدو» جدي
السابع في معطفه الجلدي يُساق الى
الموت أو المنفى
ناديتك : ألبرتي !
فأجاب : الشعرُ
وآخر طفل في المنفى يبكي الوطن الأَم
و يبكي مدريد°

In the nation / the exile, building cities for love.
The poetry / the lightning / the music answered.
The last giant cries in his coat,
The Spanish rain dries on the trees of the forest.
Sick, alone, Machado dies at dawn
All the suffering of the Spaniards returns to give birth to:
This blue fire: The books / symphonies / poetry /
Paintings.
We stood. I called you: Alberti!
The child / man / poetry answered me
"Rome was searching for Rome" in a secret leaflet
Or in the eye of a woman
Examining a sky which did not rain
Or in a glass of wine which had never been touched.
Rome was rising from beneath its ruins.
We stood under the column of light
We saw the flame of the dead, exiled
Spanish poets: Lorca, Machado
We saw the Arab coming from Toledo,
My seventh grandfather in his leather coat
Driven to his death or exile
I called you: Alberti!
Your poetry responded and
The last child in exile, crying for the motherland
Crying for Madrid.

روما موصدة الأبواب : خريف وحشي يتسترُ
خلف قناع الصمت المتفجر : برداً وعويلاً وضراعات ملاك
في الأسمالْ

شعري أورثني : هذا الفقر القاتل : هذا
الحب : اللهب : السيف القتالْ
سيحز به عنقي يوماً من أجل الفقراءْ

فليسقط شعراء ملوك العصر الحجري ، الببغاواتْ
وليسقط شعراء الجنرالاتْ

حبي دمرني
روما دمرها الزلزال

II

The doors of Rome are closed: a wild autumn
Hides behind the mask of explosive silence:
Cold, wailing, supplications of an angel in tatters.

III

From my poetry I inherited: this deadly poverty,
This love, this flame, this murderous sword
With which my throat will be cut one day
For my support of the poor.

IV

Down with the poets of the Stone Age kings,
The parakeets,
Down with the poets of the generals.

V

My love destroyed me
The earthquake destroyed Rome.

قلت : سلاماً للبحر الأبيض
قلت : سلاماً للغابات
لكن المنفيين الموتى كانوا، في كل مكان، بالمرصاد

روما نائمة : وأنا أتنصت للفجر القادم من خلف الأبواب

ناديتك : ألبرتي
فأجابت : صيحات المنفيين الأسبان
في كل بقاع الأرض المحكوم بها ، بالموت على الانسان

□   □   □

VI

I said: Peace to the White Sea
I said: Peace to the forests
But the dead exiled were lying in wait
Everywhere.

VII

Rome is asleep:
I am listening to the dawn
Coming from behind the doors.

VIII

I called you: Alberti!
I was answered by the cries of the exiled Spaniards
From every land
Where man is condemned to death.

* * *

قراءة في كتاب
الطواسين للحلاج

ــ ١ ــ

أصرخ في ليل القارات الست ، أقرب وجهي من سور الصين ، وفي نهر النيل أموت غريقاً ، كل متون الأهرامات معي ، ومراثي المعبودات ، أموت وأطفو : منتظراً دقات الساعات الرملية في برج الليل المائل ، أبني وطناً للشعر ، أقرب وجهي من وجه البناء الأعظم، أسقط في فخ الكلمات المنصوبة يُبنى حولي سورٌ ، يعلو السور و يعلو : كتبٌ ووصايا تلتف حبالاً ، أصرخ مذعوراً في أسفل قاعدة السور . لماذا يا أبت أنفى في هذا الملكوت؟ لماذا تأكل لحمي قطط الليل الحجري الضارب في هذا النصف المظلم من كوكبنا؟ ولماذا صمت البحر؟ الانسان المفعم موتاً في هذا المنفى ؟ هذا عصر شهود الزور ، وهذا عصر مسلات ملوك البدو الخصيان . أقرب وجهي من وطن الشعر : أرى آلاف التعساء المنبوذين وراء الأسوار الحجرية. في منتصف الليل يغيب النجم القطبي و ينبح كلبٌ قمر الموت . لماذا يا أبت صمت الانسان ؟

Reading From The Book
Of Al-Tawasin By Al-Hallaj

I.

I cry in the night of the six continents. I bring my face close to the Great Wall of China. In the Nile I drown to death, taking with me all the inscriptions of the pyramids and all the elegies of beloved women. I die and I drift: waiting for the sifting of sands in the hourglasses in the tilted tower of the night. I build a nation for poetry. I bring my face close to the great mason. I fall in the trap made of words. A wall is built around me, it rises and rises: books and commandments coil around me like ropes. I shout, terrified, at the base of the wall. Why, my Lord, am I exiled in this kingdom? Why do the cats of the petrified nights enveloping this half of our planet devour my flesh? And why this silence from the sea? Why is man crammed with death in this exile? This is the age of the false witnesses, the age of obelisks of castrated bedouin kings. I bring my face close to the nation of poetry. I see thousands of rejected, desperate people behind the stony walls. In the middle of the night the polar star disappears. A dog barks at the fatal moon. Why, O Lord, this silence of Man?

من تحت مسلات طغاة العالم
من تحت رماد الأزمان
من خلف القضبان
أصرخ في ليل القارات، أقدم حبي قربان
للوحش الرابض في كل الأبواب

أجيال وقوافل
أمم وممالك
أهلكها الطوفان

واحـدة بـعـد الأخـرى ، تـرتـفـع الأيـدي في وجـه الطـغـيـان
لكن سيوف السلطان
تقطعها ، واحدة بعد الأخرى ، في كل مكان

فلماذا ، يا أبت ، لم ترفع يدك السمحاء ؟

II

From beneath the obelisks of the tyrants of this world,
From beneath the ashes of the centuries,
From behind the bars,
I cry in the night of the continents,
I give my love as an offering
To the wild beast waiting at all doors.

III

Generations and caravans
Nations and kingdoms
Perished in the deluge.

IV

One after the other, hands rise in the face of tyranny
But the swords of the sultan
Cut them one after the other
Everywhere.

V

Why, then, my Lord, did you not raise
Your clement hand?

ثورات الفقراء‟
يسرقها ، في كل الأزمان ، لصوص الثورات‟

« زاباتا » كان مثالاً ومئات الأسماء الأخرى
في قاموس القديسين الشهداء‟

فلماذا ، يا أبت ، صُلِب الحلاجُ ؟

في أحــواض الــزهــر وفي غــابــات طــفــولــة حبـي ، كـان
الحـلاج رفـيـقـي في كـل الأسـفار ، وكـنـا نقـتـسم الخـبـز
ونكـتـب أشـعـاراً عــن رؤيـا الفقراء المنبوذين جيـاعـاً
في مـلـكـوت البـنـاء الأعـظـم ، عـن سر تمـرد هـذا
الانـسـان المـتـحـرق شـوقـاً للـنـور، المـحـنـي الـرأس
الى الـسـلـطـان الجـائـر . كـان الحـلاج يـعـود مـريـضـاً
ويـنـام سنيناً ويموت كثيراً ويـهز القضبان الحجرية
في كـل سـجـون الـعـالـم . قـال الحـلاج : «وداعاً»

VI

Thieves of revolutions
Steal revolutions of the poor
In all ages.

VII

Zapata was an example of hundreds of other names
In the register of saints and martyrs.

VIII

Why, my Lord, was Al-Hallaj crucified?

IX

In the flower beds and in the forests of the childhood of my love, Al-Hallaj was my companion on all voyages, we shared bread and wrote poetry about visions of the hungry, abandoned poor, in the kingdom of the great mason, about the secret of the rebellion of this man burning with desire for the light, his head bowed before the tyrant. Al-Hallaj returned sick, slept for years, died many times, and shook the stoney bars in all prisons of the world. Al-Hallaj said, "Farewell," and the

فاختفت الأحواض . وداعاً ! غابات طفولة حبي
سيصير الماء دموعاً والموت رحيلاً في هذا المنفى
هذا عصر شهود الزور ، وهذا عصر مسلات ملوك
البدو الخصيان ــ الدول الكبرى ــ الجنرالات ــ
الآلات . لماذا يا أبت لم ترفع يدك السمحاء
بوجه الشر القادم من كل الأبواب ؟ لماذا تُنفى
الكلمات ؟ يصير الحب عذاباً ؟ والصمت عذاباً ؟
في هذا المنفى ، وتصير الكلمات
طوق نجاةٍ
للغرقى في هذا اليم المسكون بفوضى الأشياء ؟

— ١٠ —

كل الفقراء اجتمعوا حول الحلاج وحول النار
في هذا الليل المسكون بحمى شيء ما ، قد
يأتي أولا يأتي من خلف الأسوارْ

□   □   □

174

flower beds disappeared. Farewell! Forests of the childhood of my love! Water will change into tears, death into departure in this exile. This is the age of the false witness, this is the age of the obelisks of the castrated Bedouin kings / the great powers / the generals / the machines. Why, my Lord, did you not raise your clement hand in the face of the evil coming from all the doors?
Why are words exiled? Why does love become suffering,
The silence a torture in this exile, and
the words
life buoys
for those drowned by this wave full of the anarchy of things?

X

All the poor gathered around Al-Hallaj,
Around the fire
In this night haunted by the fever of something
Which might or might not
Come from behind the walls.

* * *

الموت والقنديل

‫ـ ١ ـ‬

صيحاتك كانت فأس الحطاب الموغل في غابات اللغة العذراء، وكانت: ملكاً اسطورياً. يحكم في مملكة العقل الباطن والأصقاع الوثنية، حيث الموسيقى والسحر الأسود والجنس، وحيث الثورة والموت: قناع الملك الأسطوري، الممتقع الوجه وراء زجاج نوافذ قصر الصيف، وكانت: عربات الحرب الآشورية تحت الأبراج المحروقة، كانت صيحاتك صوت نبي يبكي تحت الأسوار المهدومة: شعباً مستلباً مهزوماً كانت برقاً أحمر في مدن العشق أضاء تماثيل الربات وقاع الآبار المهجورة. كانت صيحاتك: صيحاتي وأنا أتسلق أسوار المدن الأرضية، أرحل تحت الثلج، أواصل موتي في الأصقاع الوثنية، حيث الموسيقى والثورة والحب. وحيث الله

‫ـ ٢ ـ‬

لغة الأسطورة
تسكن في فأس الحطاب الموغل في غابات اللغة العذراء
فلماذا رحل الملك الاسطوري الحطاب؟

Death and the Lamp

I

Your cries were the axe of the woodcutter deeply penetrating the virgin forests of language: a legendary king ruling a subconscious kingdom and pagan regions where there exist music, black magic, sex, revolution and death: the mask of the legendary king, his face pale behind the window panes of the summer palace: your cries were: Assyrian war chariots at the foot of burned towers. Your cries were the voice of a prophet crying at the foot of destroyed walls: a people alienated and defeated. Your cries were red lightning in the cities of love, illuminating the statues of goddesses and the bottom of the abandoned wells. Your cries were my cries while I scaled the walls of the earthy cities, departing under the snow, continuing my death in the pagan countries where there exist music, revolution, love and God.

II

The language of the myth
Lives in the axe of the woodcutter, deeply penetrating
The virgin forests of language
Why did the legendary woodcutter king depart?

مات مغني الأزهار البرية،
مات مغني النار
مـات مـغـنـي عـربـات الحـرب الآشـوريـة تحت الاسوار

صيحاتك كانت صيحاتي
فلماذا نتبارى في هذا المضمار؟
فسباق البشر الفانين ، هنا ، أتعبني
وصراع الاقدار

كان الروم أمامي وسوى الروم ورائي ، وأنا كنتُ
أميل على سيفي منتحراً تحت الثلج — وقبل أفول
النجم القطبي وراء الأبراج
فلماذا سيف الدولة ولّى الأدبارْ؟

ها أنذا عار عُريَّ سماء الصحراءِ
حزينٌ حزنَ حصان غجري
مسكون بالنارْ

III

The wild flower singer died
The fire singer died
The singer of the Assyrian war chariots died
Under the walls.

IV

Your cries were my cries
Our rivalry is pointless
I am tired of mortal competition
And the struggle of destinies.

V

The Romans were in front of me
And the non-Romans behind me
I leaned on my sword, committing suicide under the snow
before the polar star setting behind the towers.
Why did Sayf Al-Dawlah retreat?

VI

Here I am
Naked like the desert sky
Sad like a gypsy horse
Haunted by fire.

— ٧ —

وطني المنفى
منفايَ الكلماتْ

— ٨ —

صار وجودي شكلاً
والشكل وجوداً في اللغة العذراء°

— ٩ —

لغتي صارت قنديلاً في باب الله°

— ١٠ —

أرحل تحت الثلج ، أواصل موتي في الأصقاع

VII

Exile is my homeland
Words are my exile.

VIII

My being became a form
The form became a being in the virgin language.

IX

My language became a lamp
At God's door.

X

I depart in the snow
Following the route of my death.

أيتها الاسحار القطبية ، ياصوت نبي يبكي ، يارعداً
في الـزمـن الأرضي المتـفـجـر حبـاً . يانـار الأ بـداع .
لماذا رحـل الملك الأسطوريُّ الحطـاب ليـترك هذي
الـغـابـات طـعـامـاً للنـار ؟ لماذا ترك الشـعـراء
خنـادقـهـم ؟ ولمـاذا سـيـف الدولة ولّى الأدبار؟ الروم
أمـامـي كـانـوا وسـوى الـروم ورائـي وأنـا كـنـت أمـيـل
على سـيـفـي مـنـتـحـراً تحت الثلج وقبل أفول النجم
القطبيِّ وراء الأ براج . صرختُ : تعالوا !
لـغـتـي صـارت قـنـديـلاً في بـاب الله . حـيـاتـي
فـرت مـن بين يـدي ، صـارت شـكـلاً والـشـكـلُ
وجوداً .
فخذوا : تاج الشوك وسيفي
وخذوا : راحلتي ،
قطرات المطر العالق في شَعري ،
زهرةَ عباد الشمس
الواضعة الخد على خدي ،
تذكاراتِ طفولة حبي ،
كتبي ، موتي
فسيبقى صوتي
قنديلاً في باب الله

□   □   □

XI

O polar dawns! O voice of crying prophet, O thunder in the earthly time, exploding with love. O fire of creation. Why did the legendary woodcutter king depart leaving these forests fuel for the fire? Why did the poets leave their trenches? Why did Sayf Al-Dawlah retreat? The Romans were in front of me and the non-Romans were behind me. I leaned on my sword, committing suicide under the snow, before the setting of the polar star behind the towers. I cried: Come! My language became a lamp at God's door. My life slipped through my hands, it became a form. The form became a being.

Take the crown of thorns and my sword
Take my steed
The drops of rain clinging to my hair
The sunflower which presses her cheek in mine
Take the memories of the childhood of my love
My books, my death
My voice will remain, a lamp
At the door of God.

* * *

صورة جانبية
لعاشق الدب الأكبر

- ١ -

كان اذا ماعاد من أسفاره ،
أراهُ تحت الثلج
في الليلِ
يسيرُ
حاسر الرأس ، وحيداً ،
فاذا ناديتهُ
أجاب في ابتسامةٍ غامضةٍ
مختفياً في الليل والريح
وفي داخله ، مواصلاً عذابه اليومي والرحيلْ
للبحث عن قارة حب طُمرتْ
تحت نديف الثلج والعويلْ
منتفضاً على رصيف الشارع الأبيض في معطفه الطويل
كأن ألف سنةٍ مرت عليه وهو في داخلهِ
محترقاً يرحل أو يعود
منتظراً علامة جديدة تظهر في غياهب السماء
أو اشارة تلمع في المجهولْ

184

Portrait of the Lover of the Great Bear

I

When he returned from his voyages
I saw him walking under the snow
In the night
Alone, bare headed,
And if I called him
He would respond with a vague smile
Disappearing in the night and the wind
And within himself
He continued his daily suffering and departure
In search of a continent of love
Covered by the flakes of snow, and wailing.
In his long coat, he stood on the white sidewalk
As if one thousand years had passed
Since he departed and returned, burning within himself
Waiting for a new sign to appear in the depths of the sky
Or a shining spark in the unknown.

كان شهاباً دامياً
يعود من أسفاره محترقاً مقروزْ

كان اذا ما عاد : لا أعرف من أين أتى
وأين كان ذلك المسحوزْ

كنتُ : أراهُ
فاذا ناديته ، أجاب في ابتسامةٍ غامضةٍ
مختفياً في النور والديجوزْ

□   □   □

II

Bloody meteor
Returning from his voyages
Burning cold.

III

When he returned, the enchanted:
I did not know from whence he came
Nor the route he was following.

IV

I saw him
And when I called him
He responded with a vague smile
Disappearing in the light and the darkness.

* * *

القصيدة الاغريقية

‏- ١ -

قـالت: مـا أقسى ، حين يغيبُ النجم ، عذابَ العاشق
أو حين يمـوت البحر . انتظريني : قال المجنون : وظلي
ميـتة بين المـوتى واقـتربي من ضوء الشـمعة ان
الله يرانـا و يرى وجهي الخائف مقترباً من وجهك
محموماً تحت نقاب الدمع . اقتربي ، فدمـوعك
في شـفـتي ملح البحر وطعم رغيف الخبز . انتظريني :
قال المجنون

‏- ٢ -

كـانت أغصـان السـرو وأشجار الدفلى تخفـي عني
مـدنـاً ونجومـاً ، تـسبح في عطر بـنفسج ليل يصعد
مـن أغـوار القـلب الانسـاني ، وكـانت امرأة عارية
فـوق حصـان تضحك في العاصفة . انتظريني ! لكن
البـحر الميت غطاها بالأعشاب وبالزبد المتطاير
في الريح . اقتربي : ناداها ، لكن صهيل حصان
البحر الأسطوري تمزق فوق صخور الشاطىء ، وانطلقت
بـضفائرها الذهـبية ، تعدو عـارية : آلهة الشعر
المجنون الى «دلفي» تبكي أقدار الشعراء .

The Greek Poem

I

She said: How severe was the lover's suffering when the star disappeared and the sea died. Wait for me, the madman said: and remain dead among the dead and approach with the light of the candle. God sees us and sees my frightened face close to your feverish face beneath the veil of tears. Come close, your tears bring the salt of the sea and the taste of bread to my lips. Wait for me, the madman said.

II

The branches of the cypress and oleander trees hid from me cities and stars which swam in the scent of night violets rising from the depth of the human heart, and a naked woman on a horse, laughed in the storm. Wait for me! But the dead sea covered her with grass and foam flying in the wind. Come close, he called her, but the neighing of the horse of the legendary sea scattered over the rocks on the shore. She ran naked with her golden tresses: the gods of crazy poetry ran to Delphi lamenting the fate of the poets.

— ٣ —

كانت في الفجر تمشط شَعرَ الأمواج
وتداعب أوتار القيثار

— ٤ —

كانت بضفائرها الذهبية ترقص عارية تحت الأمطار

— ٥ —

دهمتني ، وأنا في منتصف الدرب الى «دلفي»
صاعقــةٌ خضراء

— ٦ —

كنا أربعة : أنا والموسيقي الأعمى
ودليلي
ومغني آلهة « الأولمب » الحكماء

— ٧ —

حملتني في البحر « الايجي » الى « دلفي » أشرعة
الفجر البيضاء

III

At dawn she was combing the hair of the waves
And stroking the lyre strings.

IV

She was dancing naked with her golden tresses in the rain.

V

A green storm overtook me when I was halfway to Delphi.

VI

We were four: the blind musician,
My guide,
The chanter of the wise Olympian Gods,
And me.

VII

On the Aegean Sea
The white sails of dawn
Carried me to Delphi.

— ٨ —

وضعوني في باب المعبد أخرسَ مشلولاً
وضعوا فوق جبيني زهرة عباد الشمس
وغطوني برداء

— ٩ —

قالوا : انطق باسم الحبِ
وباسم الله
وتكلم واقرأ هذا اللوح المحفوظ وراء المحرابْ

— ١٠ —

شَقّ ملاك صدري
أخرَجَ من قلبي حبةَ مسك سوداءْ

— ١١ —

قال : اقرأ : فقرأت وصايا آلهة الشعر المكتوبِ
على الألواح
صَعَدتْ كلماتي من بئر شقاء العشاق الشهداءْ

VIII

They put me at the temple's gate
Mute, paralyzed
Over my forehead they put a sunflower
And covered me with a gown.

IX

They said: Utter in the name of love
And in the name of God
Speak and read this preserved tablet behind the prayer niche.

X

An angel opened my chest
He removed from my heart
A grain of black musk.

XI

He said: Read!
I read the commandments of the gods of poetry which were
Written on the tablets.
My words rose from the deadly well of the martyred lovers.

كانت تستلقي بضفائرها الذهبية عارية فوق رمال
الـشـاطــىء تـبـكـي عـنـد مـغـيـب الـنـجـم :
حصان البحر الأسطوري
وترسم في الأفق دوائرَ حمراء وتهمس للريح : اشتعلي
يـانـار الحب ، وكُوني شـارة هذا الليل الأ بدي
القادم مـن أطـلال المـدن الاغريقيـة ، كوني مغزل
نـار قميص الفجر الشاحب، كوني مفتاح الباب المغلق
واشتعلي حباً يا قطرات المطر المتساقط في
كل الغاباتْ
كانت ترسم فوق الرمل عيوناً وشفاه
و يداً تستجدي قطرات المطر الخضراء ٠
قالت : فلـنـرحلْ : قـال المـجـنـون : انتظري ، ظلي
ميـتـة بين الموتى ، واقتـربـي مـن ضـوء الشـمـعـة ،
ان الله يرانا و يرى وجهي الخائف مقترباً من
وجهك محموماً تحت نقاب الدمع . انتظري :
قال المجنونْ

منحتني آلهة الشعر الصافي
وأنا في درب العودة من « دلفي »
البركاتْ
وسلاحَ الكلماتْ

□

XII

She was lying nude with her golden braids on the sand of the shore, crying when the star sets for the horse of the legendary sea and drawing red circles on the horizon and whispering to the wind: Burn! Oh flame of love, be a sign of this eternal night coming from the ruins of Greek cities, be a spindle of fire for the pale dawn's shirt, be the key to the closed door. Burn in love, O drops of rain falling in every forest. She was drawing in the sands eyes and lips and her hand begging for the green drops of rain, she said: Let's depart! The madman said: Wait, remain dead among the dead and approach the light of the candle. God sees us and sees my frightened face approaching your feverish face under the veil of tears. Wait, said the madman.

XIII

On my way back from Delphi
The Gods of pure poetry
Gave me the blessing
And the power of the word.

* * *

أولد وأحترق بحبي

ـ ١ ـ

تستيقظ « لارا » في ذاكرتي :
قطاً تترياً ، يتربص بي ، يتمطى ، يتثاءب ،
يخدش وجهي المحموم ويحرمني النوم .
أراها في قاع جحيم المدن القطبية
تشنقني بضفائرها
وتعلقني مثل الأرنب فوق الحائط
مشدوداً في خيط دموعي .
أصرخ : « لارا »
فتجيب الريح المذعورة : « لارا »
أعدو خلف الريح
وخلف قطارات الليلِ
واسأل عاملة المقهى
لايدري أحد
أمضي
تحت الثلج وحيداً
أبكي حبي العاثر
في كل مقاهي العالم
والحانات

I Am Born and Burn in My Love

I

In my memory Lara awakens:
A tartar cat lying in wait
Stretching, yawning
Clawing my burning face depriving me of sleep.
I see her in the bottom of the hell of the polar cities
Hanging me with her tresses,
Suspending me like a hare upon the wall
Fettered by the string of my tears.
I shout: Lara!
The frightened wind replies: Lara!
I run behind the wind and
Behind the trains of the night
I ask the cafe waitress for news of her
But no one knows.
Beneath the snow
Alone I leave
Wailing my stumbling love
In all cafes and taverns of the world.

في لوحات «اللوفر» والأ يقونات
في أحزان عيون الملكات
في سحر المعبودات
كانت « لارا » تحت قناع الموت الذهبي
وتحت شعاع النور الغارق في اللوحات
تدعوني
فأقرب وجهي منها ،
محموماً أبكي
لكن يدأ تمتد، فتسمح كل اللوحات
وتخفي كل الأ يقونات
تاركة فوق قناع الموت الذهبي
بصيصاً من نور
لنهار مات

«لارا ! رحلتْ»
«لارا ! انتحرت»
قال البواب وقالت جارتها،
وانخرطت ببكاء حار
قالت أخرى : «لايدري أحد ،
حتى الشيطان»

II

In the paintings at the Louvre and in the icons
In the sadness of the queen's eyes
In the enchantment of adored women
Lara dwelled beneath the golden mask of death
Beneath the beams of light drowned in the paintings,
Calling me
I bring my face towards her, feverishly crying
But a hand stretches
Erasing all paintings
Concealing all icons
Leaving over the golden mask of death
A ray of light from a day that died.

III

"Lara departed!"
"Lara killed herself!"
Said the doorman and her neighbor
Who broke into hot tears.
Another neighbor said: "No one knows,
Not even the devil."

أرمي قنبلة تحت قطار الليل المشحون
بأوراق خريف في ذاكرتي ،
أزحف بين الموتى ،
أتلمس دربي
في أوحال حقول لم تحرث
أستنجد بالحرس الليلي
لأ وقف في ذاكرتي :
هذا الحب المفترس الأعمى
هذا النور الأسود ،
محموماً أبكي تحت المطر المتساقط
أطلق في الفجر على نفسي النارْ

منفياً في ذاكرتي
محبوساً في الكلمات
أشرد تحت الأمطار

أصرخ : « لارا ! »
فتجيب الريح المذعورة : « لارا ! »

IV

I throw a bomb under the train of the night
Loaded with the leaves of an autumn in my memory
I crawl among the dead
Groping my way
In the muddy untilled fields
I seek the help of the night guards
To stop:
This ravishing blind love,
This black light in my memory.
I cry feverishly under the falling rain
I shoot myself at dawn.

V

Exiled in my memory,
Imprisoned in words,
I flee under the rain.

VI

I cry: Lara!
The frightened wind replies: Lara!

في قصر الحمراء
في غرفات حريم الملك الشقراوات
أسمع عوداً شرقياً و بكاء غزال
أدنو مبهوراً
من هالات الحرف العربي
المضفور بآلاف الأزهار
أسمع آهات :
كانت « لارا » تحت الأقمار السبعة
والنور الوهاج
تدعوني ، فأقرب وجهي منها ،
محموماً أبكي ،
لكن يداً تمتد ، فتقذفني في بئر الظلمات
تاركة فوق السجادة قيثاري
و بصيصاً من نور
لنهار مات

«لم تترك عنواناً»
قال مدير المسرح وهويبط الكلمات

VII

In Alhambra
In the chambers of the blond concubines of the king
I hear the sound of an eastern lute and the cry of a gazelle,
I draw near, breathless and dazzled
By the glory of Arabic words
Interlaced with thousands of flowers
I hear rapturous sighs:
Lara was under the seven moons
And below the blazing light
Calling me,
I bring my face towards her
Crying feverishly
But a hand extends,
Throwing me into an abyss of darkness
Leaving my lyre on the carpet
And a ray of light from a day that died.

VIII

"She left no address,"
Said the theatre manager
Elongating his words.

تسقط في غابات البحر الأسود أوراق الأشجارْ
تنطفىء الأضواء
و يرتحل العشاق
وأظل أنا وحدي ، أبحث عنها ،
محموماً أبكي تحت الأمطار

أصرخ : «لارا!»
فتجيب الريح المذعورة : «لارا»
في كوخ الصياد

أرسم صورتها فوق الثلج ،
فيشتعل اللون الأخضر في عينيها
والعسليُّ الداكن ،
يدنو فمها الكرزيُّ الدافىء من وجهي ،
تلتحم الأ يدي بعناق أبدي
لكن يداً تمتد ، فتمسح صورتها ،
تاركة فوق اللون المقتول
بصيصاً من نورِ لنهارٍ ماتْ

IX

The leaves of the trees
Fall in the forests of the Black Sea.
Lights turn off
The lovers depart.
I remain alone searching for her
Feverishly crying under the rain.

X

"Lara!" I cry.
"Lara," the frightened wind replies,
"Is in the fisherman's cottage."

XI

I draw her image on the snow
The green and the honeybrown in her eyes sparkle
Her warm, cherry-red mouth draws near my face
Our hands join in eternal embrace
But a hand extends
Blotting out her image,
Leaving on the slain colors
A ray of light from a day that died.

شمس حياتي غابت :
لا يدري أحد .
الحب وجود أعمى ووحيد .
مامن أحد يعرف في هذا المنفى أحداً .
الكل وحيدٌ .
قلب العالم من حجر
في هذا المنفى الملكوت

□   □   □

XII

My life's sun has disappeared:
Nobody knows
Love is blind lonely existence
No one knows another in this exile.
All are alone
The world's heart is made of stone
In this kingdom of exile.

* * *

قمر شيراز

ــ ١ ــ

أجـرح قـلبـي ، أسقي من دمـه شعري ، تتألق جوهرة في قـاع النـهر الانـسـانـي ، تـطير فـراشـات حـمر ، تولد مـن شعـري : امـرأة حـامـلـة قـمـراً شيرازياً في سنبلةٍ من ذهب مضفوراً ، يـتـوهج في عـيـنـيـها عـسـل الـغـابـاتَ وحزن النـار الأبـديـة ، تنـبت أجنـحة في اللـيل لهـا ، فـتـطير، لـتـوقظ شـمـساً نائـمـة في حبـات الـعـرق المتـلألىء فوق جبين العاشق ، في حزن الألـوان المخبـوءة في اللـوحـات : امـرأة حـامـلـة قـمـراً شيرازياً ، في اللـيل تـطير ، تحاصر نومي ، تجرح قلبي تـسـقي مـن دمـه شـعـري ، أتـعبد فيها : فأرى مدناً غارقة في قاع النهر النابع من عينيها ، يـتـوهج سحر عـسلي : يـقـتـل مَنْ يدنو أو يرنو أو يسبح ضد التيار: أرى كـل نسـاء الـعـالـم في واحـدة تـولد من شعـري . أتمـلـكهـا ، أسكـن فيـها ، أعبدها ، أصرخ في وجه اللـيـل ولكـن جنـاحـي يـتـكسر فوق الالوان المخبوءة في اللوحاتْ

Shiraz's Moon

I

I wound my heart, I water my poetry with its blood, a gem glows at the bottom of the human river, red butterflies flutter. Born from my poetry: a woman carrying a golden braided Shirazi moon in a chaff of wheat, in her eyes glitters the honey of the forests and the sadness of eternal fire, she sprouts wings at night and flies to awaken a sleeping sun in the shining drops of sweat on the forehead of the lover. In the sadness of the colors hidden in the paintings: a woman carrying a Shirazi moon flies at night, besieges my sleep, wounds my heart, waters with its blood my poetry, I worship and adore her: I see cities drowning in the bottom of the river springing from her eyes, a spell the color of honey glows: it kills whoever approaches, gazes or swims against the current. I see all the women of the world in one woman who is born from my poetry. I possess her, live in her, worship her, I yell in the face of the night, but my wing breaks above the hidden colors in the paintings.

مجنوناً بالنهر النابع من عينيها
بالعسل الناري المتوهج في نهر النار
أسبح ضد التيار

أكتب تاريخ الأنهار
أبدؤه بطيور الحب و بالنهر الذهبي الأشجار

بدمي يغتسل العشاق
وبشعري يبني الغرباء
في المنفى «شيراز»

أتملكها ، أسكن فيها
أعبدها
أرسم في ريشتها : مدناً فاضلة يتعبد فيها الشعراء

II

Crazed by the river flowing from her eyes,
By the fiery honey blazing in the river of fire,
I swim against the current.

III

I write the history of the rivers
I begin with the birds of love
And the river of the golden trees.

IV

The lovers wash themselves with my blood
In their exile, the strangers build Shiraz
With my poems.

V

I possess her, I dwell in her
I worship her
I draw with her brush: ideal cities
Where the poets worship.

مجنوناً بالنهر النابع من عينيها
بالسيل الجامح والفيضان
باللهب المفترس الجوعان
أسبح من غير وصول للشاطىء ، أغرق سكرانْ

أفـرد أجـنـحـتـي وأطير اليها في مـنـتـصف الليل ، أراها
نـائـمـة تحـلـم بـالقـمـر الشيرازي الأخضر فوق البـوابات
الحجرية يبكي ، يتدلى من أغصان حديقتها و يظل وحيداً
يتعبد فيها : ماكان يكون : حياتي كانت في الأرض
غـيـابـاً وحضوراً تملؤه الوحشة والترحال وأشبـاح المـوتى
كـونـي أيـتـهـا المـشـربـة الوجنة بالتـوت الأحمر والورد
الجـبلي الأ بـيـض : زادي في هـذي الرحـلـة ، كـونـي
آخـر مـنـفـى وطـن : أعبـده ، أسكـن فيـه وأمـوتْ

قولي للحب : « نعم » أو قولي « لا »

VI

Crazed by the river springing from her eyes
By the impetuous torrent and the flood
By the famished ravishing flame
I swim without reaching the shore
I drown drunk.

VII

I spread out my wings and fly to her in the middle of the night,
I see her sleeping, dreaming of the green Shirazi moon which
cries upon the stoney gates and descends from the branches of
her garden and remains alone adoring her. What was will be. My
life on earth was absence and presence filled with loneliness,
departures and the ghosts of the dead. O you whose cheeks are
full of red berries and white mountain roses, be my provision on
this journey, be the last exiled nation which I will worship, and
where I will live and die.

VIII

Say to love: "Yes" or say to love: "No."

قولي : «ارحل !» فسأرحل في الحال
قولي : «أهواك :
أو قولي : « لاأهواك »

قنديلا ذهب عيناك
و يداك شراعان

أخفي فاجعة تحت قناع الكلمات . أقول لجرحي:
«لا تبرأ» ولحزني «لا تبرد» وأقول: اغتسلوا
بدمي للعشاق

تلتهم النار : النار وتخبو أحزان العشاق الرحل
في صحراء الحب وتبقى «شيراز» ونبقى نرحل في
الليل اليها : محترقين بنار الحزن الأبدية ، تنبت
أجنحة في الفجر لنا ، فنطير، ولكنا قبل وصول الركب
اليها : نتملكها، نسكن فيها : ونعود .

IX

Say to me: Leave! And I will leave at once
Say: I love you
Or say: I don't love you.

X

Two lamps of gold are your eyes
Your hands are sails.

XI

I hide a tragedy under the mask of words.
I say to my wound: Do not heal
And to my sadness: Do not disappear
I say to the lovers: Wash yourselves with my blood.

XII

The fire devours the fire. The sadness of the wandering lovers
fades away in the desert of love. Shiraz remains and we continue
to depart at night in search of her: burning in the fire of eternal
sadness. Sprouting wings at dawn we fly but before our proces-
sion reaches her, we possess her, we live in her and we return.

وجــدونـي عـنـد يـنـابـيـع النـور قتيـلا ، وفمـي بـالتـوت
الأحمـر والـورد الجـبلي الأ بـيـض مـصـبـوغـاً وجـنـاحـي
مغروساً في النورْ

□   □   □

XIII

They found me dead at the sources of light
My mouth dyed with red berries and white mountain roses
My wings planted in the light.

* * *

حب تحت المطر

«واترلو» كان البدء ، وكل جسور العالم كانت ،

تمتد لواترلو ، لتعانقه ، لترى :

مُغتربَين التقيا تحت عمود النور ،

ابتسما ، وقفا

وأشارا لوميض البرق

وقصف السحب الرعدية .

عادا ينتظران ، ابتسما ،

قالت عيناها : « من أنت؟ »

أجاب : « أنا ! لا أدري » وبكى ،

اقتربت منه ،

وضعت يدها في يده ،

سارا تحت المطر المتساقط

حتى الفجر ،

وكانت كالطفل تغني

تقفز من فوق البرك المائية ،

تعدو هاربة وتعودُ .

شوارعُ لندن كانت

تتنهد في عمق

والفجر على الأرصفة المبتلة في عينها ،

218

Love Under the Rain

I

Waterloo was the beginning.
All bridges of the world were
Reaching for it, to embrace it, to see:
Two strangers meet
Under the column of light
They smiled and stood, pointing
To flashes of lightning
And the roar of thunder clouds.
They continued to wait and they smiled.
Her eyes asked: "Who are you?"
He replied: "I don't know," and cried.
She approached him
And placed her hand in his
They walked beneath the falling rain
Until dawn
She sang like a child,
Jumping over puddles,
Fleeing and returning.
London streets were sighing deeply
The dawn
Reflecting the wet pavement in her eyes

يتخفى في اوراق الاشجار
أجاب : «أنا ، لاأدري » وبكى .
قالت : «سأراك غداً »
عانقها ،
قبل عينها تحت المطر المتساقط
كانت كجليد الليل
تذوب حناناً تحت القبلاتْ

— ٢ —

عانقها ثانية
وافترقـــا
تحت سماء الفجر العارية السوداء

— ٣ —

كانت تبكي في داخله
سنوات طفولته الضائعة العجفاء

— ٤ —

كان يراها في الحلم كثيراً منذ سنين
كانت صورتها تهرب منه
اذا ما استيقظ
أو ناداها في الحلم

Hid in the leaves of the trees.
He answered: "I do not know," and cried.
She said: "I will see you tomorrow."
He embraced her and kissed her eyes
under the falling rain
She was like night frost,
Melting with tenderness beneath his kisses.

II

He embraced her a second time
They parted
Beneath the naked black sky of dawn.

III

The years of his lean, lost childhood
Were crying within him.

IV

For years he saw her in his dreams.
If he awoke
Or if he called her
Her image escaped him.

وكان بحمى العاشق يبحث عنها في كل مكان
كان يراها
في كل عيون نساء المدن الأرضية
بالأزهار مغطاة
و بأوراق الليمون الضارب للحمرة ،
تعدو حافية تحت الأمطار ،
تشير اليه : «تعال ورائي»
يركض مجنوناً ،
يبكي سنوات المنفى
وعذاب البحث الخائب عنها
والترحال

— ٥ —

كانت تنشب في داخله معركة بين المعبوداتْ :
واحدة ماتت قبل الحب
وأخرى بعد الحب
وأخرى في المابين
وأخرى تحت الأنقاض

— ٦ —

ثورة موتى :
كانت زلزالْ

With the fever of a lover
He searched for her in every place
He saw her
In every woman's eyes of those earthy cities,
Cloaked in flowers
And in the reddish lemon leaves
Running barefoot under the rain
Beckoning him: "Come, follow me."
Madly he ran
Crying for the years of exile
And the torture of his vain search
And endless wandering.

V

Within him raged a battle
Among the women he adored:
One died before love,
Another after love,
Another in between,
And another under the rubble.

VI

Revolution of the dead:
An earthquake.

و « تعال ورائي »
ظلت في لحم السنوات العاري
ودم الحب المُغتال
جرحاً لايُشفى
وحنيناً قتـال

كان يراها في كل الأسفارْ
في كل المدن الأرضية بين الناس
و يناديها في كل الأسماء

كانت تتخفى
في أوراق الليمون
وأزهار التفاح

«واترلو» كان البدء
وكل جسور العالم كانت تمتد
لواترلو ،
تسعى للقاء الغرباء

VII

"Come, follow me," remained
An open wound
And a deadly yearning
In the naked flesh of the years
And in the blood of the murdered love.

VIII

He saw her in all voyages
In every city on earth
Among people
Calling her by every name.

IX

She was hiding
In lemon leaves
In apple blossoms.

X

Waterloo was the beginning,
All bridges of the world were reaching toward it,
To meet the strangers.

تحت عمود النور التقيا ،
ابتسما ، وقفا
واشارا لوميض البرق
وقصف السحب الرعدية.
كانا يعتنقان

كان يمارس سحراً أسود في داخله :
«تأتي أو لا تأتي ؟ من يدري ؟ »
مجنوناً كان .

كانت في يده دمية شمع
يغرز فيها دبوساً من نار
« حبيني » قال لها ،
واتقدت عيناه
بشرارة حزن يصعد من قلب المأساة

XI

They met under the column of light,
They smiled and stood, pointing
To flashes of lightning
And the roar of thunder clouds
They were embracing.

XII

Inside himself he practiced black magic:
"Will she or won't she come? Who knows?"
Madness.

XIII

He had a wax doll in his hand
Pierced with a needle of fire
He said to her: "Love me,"
His eyes flamed
With a spark of sadness
Rising from the heart of the tragedy.

شاحبة كالوردة تحت عمود النور رآها

جاءت قبل الموعد

كانت في معطفها المطري الأزرق

قبلها من فمها

سارا

قالت : «فلنسرع!»

ضحكا، دخلا بارأ، طلبا كأسين

اقتربت منه ، وضعت يدها في يده

قالت عيناه لها : «حبيني»

غرقا في حلم :

فرآها ورأته : في أرض أخرى

تحرقها شمس الصحراء

ابتسما ، عادا من أرض الحلم

أراها صورته بلباس البدو الرحل

قالت : «من أنت؟»

أجاب: «أنا لا أدري» وبكى

كانت صحراء حمراء

تمتد وتمتد الى ماشاء الله

لتغطي خارطة الأشياء

XIV

He saw her, pale as a rose under the column of light
She had arrived early
Wearing a blue raincoat
He kissed her on the lips
They walked
She said, "Let's hurry."
They laughed, and entered a bar, ordered two drinks
She drew close to him and placed her hand in his.
His eyes said to her: "Love me."
They drowned in a dream:
He saw her and she saw him in another land
Burned by the desert sun
They smiled and returned from the land of the dream.
He showed her his picture in bedouin clothes
She said: "Who are you?"
He responded: "I do not know," and wept.
It was a red desert
Stretching to where only God knows
To cover the map of everything.

عانقها ، قبّل عينيها
لندنُ كانت تتنهد في عمق
والفجر
على الأرصفة المبتلة في عينيها
يتخفى في أوراق الأشجارْ

«عائشة : اسمي» قالت :
«وأبي ملكاً اسطورياً كان
يحكم مملكة دمرها زلزال
في الألف الثالث قبل الميلاد»

□   □   □

XV

He embraced her and kissed her eyes
London was deeply sighing
The dawn
Reflecting the wet pavement in her eyes
Hid in the leaves of the trees.

XVI

She said: "Aisha is my name.
And my father was a legendary king
Whose kingdom was destroyed by an earthquake
In the third millenium before Christ."

* * *

مملكة السنبلة
(١٩٧٩)

- النور يأتي من غرناطة
- سمفونية البعد الخامس الأولى
- مقاطع من عذابات فريد الدين العطار
- سأبوح بحبك للريح وللأشجار

The Kingdom of Grain

(1979)

233

النور يأتي من غرناطة

- ١ -

أتكور طفلاً كي أولد في قطرات المطر المتساقط فوق الصحراء العربية، لكن الريحَ الشرقية تلوى عنقي، فأعود إلى غار حِراء يتيماً، يخطفني نسر، يلقي بي تحت سماء أخرى، أتكور ثانية، لكني لا أولد أيضاً، أتخطى الوضع البشري، أدور وحيداً حول الله وحول منازله في الأرض، يلاحقني صوت كمان يعزف في الليل عليه مئات العشاق المسكونين بنار الميلاد، أحاول أن أتوقف عند الوتر المرتجف المقطوع، ولكن الموسيقى تجرفني، أصرخ عند الذروة، ايقاع مصحوب ببكاء إنساني، يندفع الآن ويخبو، موسيقي أعمى ينزف فوق الأوتار دماً، يرفع مثلي يده في صمت فراغ الأشياء، ويبحث عن شيء ضاع، يدور وحيداً حول الله، بصوت فمي أو فمه يصرخ، تحمله الذروةُ نحو قرار الموجة، يبكي تحت سماء بلاد أخرى، لكن الأوتار، تظل تلاحقني في صمت القاعة. من منا يولد في هذي الصحراء الآن

Light Comes From Granada

I

I curl up like an infant, to be reborn in the drops of rain falling on the Arabian desert, but the wind of the East twists my neck. I return an orphan to the cave of Hira'. An eagle snatches me up, releases me under another sky. I curl up once again, but this time I am not reborn. I transcend the human condition. I circle alone around God and his dwellings on earth. I am pursued by the sound of a violin made to tremble in the night by hundreds of lovers haunted by the flame of birth. I try to stop myself at the broken, vibrating string, but the music transports me. I cry out at the climax. A rhythm, accompanied by a human sob, bursts forth now and fades away. The blood of a blind musician flows over the strings. Like me, he raises his hand in the silence of the void. He searches for something lost. He circles alone around God. He cries out with the voice of my mouth or his own. The climax carries him to the trough of the wave. He weeps beneath the sky of another country. But the strings continue to pursue me in the silence of the hall. Which of us is born now in this desert?

يعـرّي الموسيقي الأعمى : جرحك أم جرحي ؟ من مّنا ينزف
فـوق الأ وتار دمـاً ؟ من منا العازف تحت الشرفات العربية في
غرناطةَ ، يبكي حباً ما ، وحبيباً ما ، و يطوف أزقتها مخموراً في
وحشة من يرحل أو يبقى ، يبدأ أوينهي رحلته ، و يقول وداعاً
لمآذن قصر الحمراء، يـدور وحيـداً، حول الله وحول منازله في
الأ رض، يـلاحـقه صوتُ كمان. لن أبحث عن أوتار أخرى ،
فغنـائي بلور حطمه في أرض الصيرورة : صوتُ غناء الانسان
الـواعد والحب المـوعود. لماذا عرباتُك في بابي تقفُ الآن ؟
وخيـلُك تصهل تحت وميـض البـرق الداهم في هذا الليل
الأسباني ؟ لماذا لم تُطلق قوسك في برج الجوزاء لكي يأخذ
وجهي شكل أبي الهول الرافض في بسمته العدمَ المجهولْ؟

ما يبقى هو هذي النار
وعذاب الشعراء

II

The blind musician uncovers: your wound or mine? Which of us is bleeding upon the strings? Which of us is playing music under the Arabian balconies at Granada, weeping over love, and a lover, wandering in the alleys, intoxicated with the desolation of someone departing or remaining, beginning or ending his journey, saying his adieus to the minarets of the Alhambra and circling alone around God and his dwellings on earth, as the music of the violin pursues him? I shall not search for other strings. My singing is a crystal shattered upon the land of change: by the singing of the promising man and by the promised love. Why do your chariots stop now at my door? And your horses neigh under the blinding flash of this Spanish night? Why do you not shoot your arrow into Gemini so that my face will take the form of the Sphinx, rejecting the unknown void with his smile?

III

All that remains
Is this fire
And the suffering of poets.

رجـل في سـفر ، يـترنح وهو يتوج امرأة بضفائرها ، و يعانقها
و يـقول لها : ياضوء الحب و يالغةً يستولدُ منها و بها ولها ، هذا
الطفل المتكور كي يولد في قطرات المطر المتساقط فوق الصحراء
العـربيـة ، لكـن الـريـح الشـرقية، تلوي عنق الطفل وتذرو
السـحب البيضاء هباء ، و يظل الرجل الطفل سنيناً في سفرٍ،
مايبقى : يهدمه أو يبنيه الشعراءُ و يقول لها : من متا الخاسرُ في
لعبة هذا الحب الهدامْ؟

ولماذا يسكنني هذان الضدان ؟

« لن يبني بيتاً ، من لابيت له الآن »

لكـن المـرأة تبكي غربتها في منفى لغة الرمز ، تخون و يسقط
تاج الذهب المضفور على قدميها . صوت كمان يعزف في الليل
عـليـه مئـات العشـاق، يلاحقني ، أتوقف عند الوتر المرتجف
المقطوع ولكن الموسيقى تجرفني ، أصرخ عند الذروة : من متا ،
غرناطة ، خان وباعَ عذابَ الشعراءْ وسنابل قمح الفقراء ؟
من متا مات على الأسوار ؟

IV

A traveling man totters as he crowns a woman with her braids
and embraces her saying: O light of love, O language through
which, from which and for which is born this child who curls up
to be reborn in the drops of rain falling on the Arabian desert.
But the wind of the East twists the child's neck and scatters the
white clouds in vain. For years the man-child continues his jour-
neys. What is left: destroyed or built by the poets. He says to
her: Which of us is the loser in this destructive game of love?
And why am I possessed by these two contradictions? "He who
has no house will never build one." But the woman weeps in
her isolation in the exile of symbolic language. She betrays, and
the braided crown of gold falls around her feet. I am pursued by
the music of a violin made to tremble in the night by hundreds
of lovers. I stop at the broken, vibrating string, but the music
transports me. I cry out at the climax. Which of us, O Granada,
has betrayed and sold the suffering of the poets and the wheat
kernels of the poor? Which of us has died upon the walls?

ايقاع مصحوب ببكاء إنساني ، يندفع الآن ويخبو موسيقي
أعمى ينزف فوق الأ وتار دماً ، يرفع مثلي يده في صمت فراغ
الأشياء ، و يبحث عن شيء ضاع ، يدور وحيداً حول الله ،
بصوت فمي أو فمه يصرخ : مَنْ منّا خان الآخر ؟ من منّا حباً
مات ؟

— ٥ —

المرأة ظلـتْ تبكي في منفاها الأ بـدي وتبكي النافورةُ
في قصر الحمراء.

□   □   □

A rhythm accompanied by a human sob bursts forth now and fades away. The blood of a blind musician flows over the strings. Like me, he raises his hand in the silence of the void. He searches for something lost. He circles alone around God. He cries out with the voice of my mouth or his own: Which of us has betrayed the other? Which of us has died of love?

V

The woman weeps in her eternal exile
The fountain weeps in the Alhambra.

* * *

سمفونية البعد الخامس الأ ولى

— ١ —

مابين ليالي القطب البيضاء ونار خرائب هذا الفجر الدامي،
تتوقف أحياناً مركبة حاملةً جثثاً وطيوراً ميتة، تنزل منها سيدة
في عمر الوردة، تمضي في جوف الليل إلى غابات البحر الأسود،
يتبعها و يتوجها نجم أسطوري أخضر، وتحاول أن تتوقف
ثانيةً، لكن الريح تناديها في جوف الغابات، فتمضي تاركة
فوق مدار الأرض القطبي: المدنَ، الحانات، قواميس الشعراء
العشاق، وعائدة للمركبة — السيدة المجهولة — لكني أتبعها
وأحاول أن أستبقيها في خوف الطفل وذعر الملاح بُعيد غياب
النجم القطبي على أطراف الأقيانوس المهتاج ولكني أسقط
تحت ضباب الأشجار، وألمح من بين أصابع كفي في الأفق
رحيل المركبة — السيدة المجهولة، نقطة ضوء أسود في قاع إناء
الأفلاك السيارة، تخبو وتجف لتبقى فيها نارٌ لاتخبو في القاعْ.
وأوارُ قتالْ
أحمله كل مساء وجعاً وضياعاً في الحانات فاذا جن الليل،
ينام، ليصحو ثانية في جوف الأسحار حباً مفترساً، أعمى،
لايُشفى أو يُروى أو يُغتال.

First Symphony of the Fifth Dimension

I

Between the white nights of the Pole and the ruinous fire of this bloody dawn, there sometimes stops a vessel loaded with corpses and dead birds. A lady in the flower of life descends from it. She plunges into the night, toward the forests of the Black Sea. A fabulous green star follows her and crowns her. She tries to stop a moment, but the wind in the depths of the forests beckons to her. She advances, leaving on the polar circle of the earth: cities, taverns, lexicons of the poets of love, and returns to the ship—the unknown lady—but I follow her, and with the child's fear and the navigator's terror, I try to hold her back, just as the polar star has set on the borders of the raging ocean. But I collapse under the fog of the trees, and from between the fingers of my hand I discern on the horizon the departure of the vessel—the unknown lady—a point of black light at the bottom of the basin of shooting stars, fading away and drying up until nothing remains but an undying flame in the depths. I carry with me every evening to the taverns a deadly thirst, pain and a sense of loss, which sleep with the madness of night but return with the dawn like a blindly voracious love, incurable, insatiable, beyond the reach of death.

هأنذا أرحل في نومي، ما بين ليالي القطب البيضاء ونار
خرائب هذا الفجر الدامي، أتوقف أحياناً في بار أو مقهى فجرٍ
أتنفس في عمق، أزفر، أتوقف عند نوافذ هذا البيت وذاك،
أقول لنفسي، من يدري قد تهبط في هذي المرة حافية تحت
الأمطار بوارسو أو باريس، أو هي نائمة خلف نوافذ
هذا البيت المهجور، سأسأل عمال محطات المترو، من
يدري، قد تفتح نافذة في هذا الفجر، وتهبط منها
نحو الشارع في عمر الوردة، غامرة بضفائرها وجهي،
وأقول لنفسي وأنا أبكي في برد الطرقات :
لماذا لم تتحدث أوراق البردية عنها ؟ ولماذا لم تترك عنواناً في
شباك بريد الليل الآتي ؟ وأحدث أشجار الشارع عنها، وأقول
لها : إني أعمى ضيّعت حياتي مابين المنفى والمنفى، أترقب
مركبة تهبط من بين أصابع كفي . مابين عذاب الشعر وموتي
هبطت مرات، لكني لم أسأل أو أتساءل في حمى دوران
الأفلاك ، لماذا تركتني أبحث عنها في كتب السحر وقاع
الآبار ؟

II

Thus I travel in my slumber, between the white nights of the Pole and the ruinous fire of this bloody dawn. At the first glimmer of day, I occasionally stop at a bar or cafe. I take a deep breath and let it out. I stop beneath the windows of one house or another, and I say to myself: Who knows? Perhaps she will come down this time, barefoot, under the rain at Warsaw or Paris, or perhaps she is asleep behind the windows of this deserted house. I will ask the subway workers about her. And who knows: perhaps at dawn she will open a window and come down from it into the street. She will come, this woman in the flower of life, to bathe my face in her braids. I say to myself, as I cry in the bitter cold of the streets: Why did the papyrus not speak of her? Why did she not leave an address at the post office of the coming night? I talk to the trees along the avenue about her. I tell them: I am blind. I have lost my life from exile to exile, waiting for a vessel to come down between my fingers. It has often fallen between the throes of poetry and my death, but I have not questioned nor have I been questioned in the febrile revolution of the planets: Why has she left me to search for her in the books of magic and in the depths of wells?

أحيـاناً ألمح ايماضاً واشارات في قاع إناء الصمت المكسور وفي
ليـل الأفلاك السيارة ، ثمة إنسان في جوف الليل يراقبني في
نجم دري آخـر ، يُرسل لي شـارات غامضة أسمعه يتنهد في
نومي ، يـقرأ أفكاري ويُسرح شعري مبتسماً ، أسمعه يتلفظ
بـاسـمي ، ويقول : تـعال إذا ما جن الليل القادم أو أعولت
الريح وراء جبـال الأ ورال، أقول له: إني أعمى ووحيد —
ينطمس الصوت وأبقى فوق رصيف محطة نومي مشدوداً في
حجر مغناطيسي مغموراً بالظلمة في قاع جحيمي . مابين
عذاب الشـعر وموتي ألمح إيماضاً واشارات أخرى من مركبة
تمضي مابين خرائب هـذا الفجر الدامي وسماء ليالي القطب
البيضاء

سيـدتي المجهـولة في جـوف الليـل تراقبـني ، تتـنهد في
حمى دوران الأفلاك .

□   □   □

III

Sometimes I perceive a dim light and signals at the bottom of the broken basin of silence, and in the night of shooting stars. There, in the depths of the night, a man lies in wait for me, sending me vague signals from a brilliant star. I hear him sigh in my slumber. Smiling, he reads my thoughts and strokes my hair. I hear him pronounce my name and say: If this next night comes to folly and the wind howls behind the Ural Mountains, you may come. I tell him: I am blind and alone. The voice falls silent and I find myself on the pavement of my sleep riveted to the magnetic rock, enveloped by the darkness in the depths of my own hell. Between the throes of poetry and my death: I perceive a dim light, and other signals, emanating from a vessel that sails between the ruins of this bloody dawn and the sky of the white nights of the Pole.

IV

In the depths of the night the unknown lady lies in wait for me and sighs in the febrile revolution of the planets.

* * *

مقاطع من عذابات
فريد الدين العطار

بادرني بالسكر، وقال: أنا الخمر وأنت الساقي، فلتصبح ياأنتَ أنا محبوبي: «يرهن خرقته للخمر و يبكي مجنوناً بالعشق»، عراه غبارٌ ـ قلبي من فرط الأسفار إليكَ ومنك، فناولني الخمر ووسدني تحت الكرمة مجنوناً ولتبحث عن ياقوت فمي تحت الأفلاك السبعة، ولتُشعل بالقبلات الظمأى في لحم الأرض حريقاً، مرآة لي كنتَ، فصرتُ أنا المرآة، أعزّيك أمامي وأرى عُريي، أبحث في سكري عنك وفي صحوي، مادامت أقداح الساقي تتحدث دون لسانْ.

يا روح عناصر هذا العالم ، يا أضواء الليل الفضية والزرقاء

هأنذا أسجد في الحضرة سكرانْ

ضيفاً لمليكة هذا الليل المسكون بروح الصهباء

أهـذي والخمر معي تهذي ، قيثار العشق ، أعريك أمامي في ألحانْ

مـا كنت أبوح بحبي ، لولم تسكب هذي الغابات الملكية خضرتها في الماء

Variations On The Suffering
Of Farid Al-Din Al-Attar

I

He was first called to drunkenness. I am the wine, he says, and you are the wine bearer. If only you could become me, O you my beloved. "He pawns his sacred cloth for wine and weeps, mad with love." My heart is covered with dust from traveling to you — from you. So serve me wine and tuck me in, mad, at the foot of the vine. Fish the rubies out of my mouth under the seven celestial spheres, and with ardent kisses, light a blaze in the flesh of the earth. For me you were a mirror, I have become the mirror. In your nakedness that I have caused, I see my nakedness. As long as the cupbearer's goblets speak without tongue, I will search for you in my drunkenness and in my lucidity.
O souls of the elements of this world, O blue and silver
lights of the night!
See how I prostrate myself, drunk in a trance.
Guest of the queen of this night haunted by the spirit of the wine.
I am raving and the wine raves with me, O guitar of love,
my nakedness cries out for yours.
I would not have confessed my love if these royal forests had not poured out their greenness into the wave.

مافي الجبة إلاّ الانسان

مرآة لي كنتَ ، فصرتُ أنا المرآة

أعـقـرُ ناقة هذا الليـل الصحراوي الأسيـان ، وأهذي
بـجوار الدن المجروح أقولُ : سيأتي عصر أو زمن يُصبح
فيه الانسان سديماً لأخيه الانسان
(ومليـكاً للأفلاك ...) السبعة ، يرهن خرقته للخمر
ويبكى مجنوناً بالعشق وتنهض عائشة من تحت الأعشاب
البـرية والأحجـار السـوداء غزالاً ذهبيـاً تـعدو وأنا أتبعها
تحت الكرمة مجنوناً ، أمسكها وأعريها وأرى عري .
مرآة لي كنت ، فصرت أنا المرآة . أقول : سيأتي ! لكن
الـريح وراء الأ بـواب تراقص أجسـاد الأشجـار العـارية
الصفراء وتُلقي بمصابيح الشعراء
في قاع الآبار
ما كنت أعري جرحي في الحضرة لولم أفقد عائشةً
في حان الأقدار
ماكنت أبوح بسري للنجم الثاقب لولاك

II

In the tunic there is man, nothing but man.

III

For me you were a mirror, I have become the mirror.

IV

I slaughter the camel of this sad Saharan night. I rave beside the fallen wounded beast and I say: The time will come when man becomes dust for his brother man (and master of the seven celestial spheres), pawning his sacred cloth for wine, weeping, mad with love. So Aisha gets up from under the wild grasses and the black stones, a fleeing golden gazelle, and I follow her, mad, under the vines, I seize her, undress her, and see my nakedness. For me you were a mirror, I have become the mirror. I say: This time will come! But the wind beyond the doors makes the naked body of the yellow trees dance, and hurls the poets' lanterns to the bottom of the well. I would not have uncovered my wound in the trance if I had not lost Aisha in the tavern of destinies. Without you, I would not have confided my secret to the shooting star.

لا غـالب إلا الخمـار ، فنـاولني الخمـر ووسـدني تحت
الكرمة مجنوناً
ولتبحث عن ياقوت فمي تحت الأفلاك

‒ ٥ ‒

حـولـك في الـنـوم أطـوف وأسـقط في كـابـوس الصحـو
الملتاث

‒ ٦ ‒

لـن أُهـــزَم حتـى آخربيت أكتبه ، فلنشرب في قبة
هذا الليل الزرقاء
حتى يدركنا الليل الأ بدي ونغفو في بطن الغبراء

‒ ٧ ‒

سأموت أنا وتموتين
فلماذا في أعراس الدنيا تبكين ؟
وتدورين ؟
يا قرة عين الساقي المجنون

The barkeeper alone is the victor, so serve me some wine, tuck me in, mad, at the foot of the vine and fish the rubies out of my mouth under the celestial spheres.

V

In my slumber, I wander around you and I fall into the nightmare of demented wakefulness.

VI

I shall not be defeated until I write the last verse of poetry, so let us drink in the blue vault of this night until the eternal night reaches us and we sleep in the belly of the earth.

VII

I shall die and you shall die
So why do you weep in the middle of life's celebrations?
Why do you do nothing but revolve, O consolation of the mad cup bearer?

سَفَرٌ لا حد له وسباق قذر في حلبات الدنيا ، والدنيا
رغم بريق نجوم الليل ، سحاب يركض مهزوماً ، يسقط
من شرفات هواها : اللص الفاتك والعبد المملوك . لماذا
نرحل ان كنا قد جئنا ؟ ولماذا قبل قطاف الورد نموت ؟
لماذا في أعراس طفولتنا نبكي ونلف بخوف وندور؟
فناولني الخمر ووسدني تحت الكرمة مجنوناً ، فالموت الحيّ
المتربص في الحانات وفي الأسواق وفي عينيْ هذا الساقي
يُغمد في صدري سكيناً ، أصرخ ، لكني من فرط الأسفار
إليك ومنك ، أُسائل في سكري عنك وفي صحوي.
فلتصبح يا أنت أنا محبوبي ، يرهن خرقته للخمر ويبكي
مجنوناً بالعشق .

مرآة لي كنت ، فصرت أنا المرآة

لا غالب إلاّ الخمّار

□   □   □

VIII

Endless voyage, corrupt race in the arenas of the world. And the world, despite the shining of the stars, is a defeated cloud, running. Falling from the balcony of its love: the ruthless thief, the eternal slave. Why do we depart when we have already arrived? Why do we die before gathering the flowers? Why do we weep in the weddings of our childhood and move in circles, wrapped with fear? So, give me the wine and tuck me under the vine, mad. The living death waits in the taverns, in the markets and in the eyes of this cup bearer, piercing a knife in my chest. I cry. But because of excessive travelling to and from you, I wonder about you in my drunkenness and lucidity. Be me, oh my love, pawning your sacred cloth, weeping, mad with love.

IX

For me you were a mirror. I have become the mirror.

X

Only the tavern keeper is victorious.

* * *

سأبوح بحبك للريح وللأشجار

— ١ —

تـقبع في غرفتك الآن وحيداً، تنهال التذكارات، فها هي ذي الدنيا :
جسد امرأة تتأوه تحتك ، مغمضة عينيها ، يسقط ثلج أسودُ فوق الخدين
فتبكي في صمت، فسنابل قمح الجسد العاري ، تكسرها ريح
مغيب ، يتوغـل في مدن لم تُولد . من أي مدار شمسي تهبط فوق
الأرض: العربات الذهبية حاملة للجسد المنفي ، بذور الابداع ونار
الخلق الأولى ؟ من أي السنوات الضوئية ، يأتي هذا الضيف الحجري
بـسلة أثمار الصيف ؟ فتبكي في صمت . من أي نهار ينبثق الفرح
الباكي وبيوت ، ليترك فوق الأوراق نجوماً وعصافير
وإلى أين تسير ؟
هذي الدنيا بعباءتها في الريح؟
امرأة حبلى في الشهر التاسع قرب البحر تصيح
تتشهى القمر الليموني النائم فوق سطوح الريف

— ٢ —

يا امرأة الهملايا وسفوح الأنديز
نامي في قاع محيط الروح
حتى ينفجر البركان و يعوي كلب الرؤيا المسعور

I Shall Reveal My Love For You
to the Wind and the Trees

I

You crouch alone now in your room. Memories wash over you. Such is life: the body of a woman sighing beneath you, eyes closed, as black snow falls on her cheeks. She cries in silence. The grains of the naked body are shattered by the wind of dusk that penetrates the unborn cities. From what solar orbit have dropped to earth: the golden chariots bringing exile to the body, the seeds of art, and the first flame of creation? From what light-year comes this stony guest with a basket of summer fruit? She cries in silence. From what day does the sorrowful joy spring forth and die, leaving stars and birds upon the leaves? And where is she going, this world with her cloak in the wind? A pregnant woman in her ninth month crying by the sea, craving the lemon-colored moon that sleeps above the roofs of houses in the countryside.

II

O woman of the Himalaya Mountains and the Andean plains,
Sleep at the bottom of the ocean of the soul
Until the volcano's eruption
Until the howling of the vision's mad dog.

‒ ٣ ‒

ربات الأقدار
يرقصن على موسيقى الجاز
في صالة رقص الأمطار

‒ ٤ ‒

ها أنت تشد الأوتار وتبكي في أعقاب طقوس الاخصاب
لبذور الخلق الأولى ، تحت رماد الأحقاب

‒ ٥ ‒

عاصفة تقتلع الأبواب
تلقي بخريطة هذي الدنيا فوق الأرض وتطفىء ضوء
المصباح

‒ ٦ ‒

ها أنت تواجه نفسك في المرآة
بقميصك نار تشتعل الآن

III

The mistresses of destiny
Dance to the rhythm of the jazz
In the dance hall of the rains.

IV

Here you are tightening the strings and crying at the fertility
Rites' conclusion
For the first seeds of creation under the ashes of time.

V

A storm rips out the gates
Hurls the map of the world to the ground and puts out the
Light of the lamp.

VI

You are facing yourself in the mirror
Now the fire catches your shirt.

يتوغل في قلبك : حزن الليل الاسباني وثلج الغابات الروسية ،
تسقط من فوق الكرسي مريضاً ، تأكلك الحمى تصرخ ، لكن
الصرخات تضيع هباء ــ النجدة ! إنسان يحترق الآن وحيداً
في غرفته ، يتشبث بالحبر و بالأ وراق. بخارى بمآذنها الزرقاء
تصلي للأنهار الوحشية في أعماق الليل وتتلو آيات زرادشت
الأشجار : ربيع شعوب يولد من حبات القمح ومن صلوات
الريح ، وأنت تصلي للشعب المأخوذ العاري من حد الماء إلى
حد الماء ْ
ترسم خارطة لعيون المعبودات وربات الأقدار
تسقط من فوق الكرسي ، مريضاً فوق الخارطة البيضاء

يا امرأة الهملايا وسفوح الأنديز ، لماذا فوق سرير
الأمطار تنام جبال الفيروز ؟

يموت الشاعر منفياً أو منتحراً أو مجنوناً أو عبداً أو خداماً في
هذي البقع السوداء وفي تلك الأقفاص الذهبية، حيث الشعب
المأخوذ العاري من حد الماء إلى حد الماء يموتُ ببطء ، تحت
سياط الارهاب ، وحيداً ، معزولاً ، منبوذاً ، محروماً قرب
الأقفاص .

VII

Penetrating your heart: The sadness of the Spanish night and the snow of the Russian forests. You fall from your chair, ill. Fever consumes you. Your cries are in vain: Help! A man is now burning alone in his room. He clings to his ink and paper. Bukhara with her blue minarets prays for the wild rivers in the depths of the night. The trees recite the verses of Zarathustra: The peoples' spring is born of the grains of wheat and of the prayers of the wind, and you are praying for the naked, dazed people from shore to shore. You are drawing a map for the eyes of worshipped women and the mistresses of destiny. You fall from the seat, ill, upon the blank map.

VIII

O woman of the Himalaya Mountains and the Andean plains, why do the turquoise mountains sleep on the bed of rains?

IX

The poet dies by suicide / exiled / madman / slave / servant in these black lands and in these gilded cages where reside the dazed, naked people from shore to shore.
Slowly, under the whips of terror alone / isolated / rejected / forbidden, he dies beside the cages.

ياامرأة : ستكون
سأبوح بحبك للريح وللأشجار
وأعيد كتابة تاريخك فوق الخارطة البيضاء

□   □   □

X

O woman who will be
I shall reveal my love for you to the wind and the trees
And I shall rewrite your history on the blank map.

* * *

بُستان عائشة (١٩٨٩)

Aisha's Orchard

(1989)

- *Elegy to Khalil Hawi*
- *From the Papers of Aisha*
- *Another Paper*
- *The Fire of Poetry*
- *False Critics*
- *The Birth in Unborn Cities*
- *The Blind Singer*
- *A Smoke Dancer*
- *The Birth*
- *Aisha's Orchard*
- *Aisha's Profile*
- *The Deceiver*
- *The Face*
- *The Great Wall of China*
- *A Woman*
- *Al-Basra*
- *The Unknown Man*
- *The Peacock*
- *The Poem*
- *A Man and a Woman*
- *A Profile of a City*
- *Secret of Fire*
- *A Conversation of a Stone*

مرثية إلى خليل حاوي

‐ ١ ‐

حين انتظرَ الشاعرْ
ماتت عائشةٌ في المنفى
نجمةَ صُبح صارتْ:
لارا وخزامى / هنداً وصفاءْ
ومليكةَ كل الملكاتْ
تمثالاً كنعانياً
نار حريقٍ في أبراج البترولِ
وفي أبيات «نشيد الانشادْ»
ودماً فوق سطور «التوراةْ»
وجباهِ لصوص الثوراتْ
صارت نيلاً وفرات
ونذورَ الفقراء
فوق جبال الأطلس،
قافية في شعر أبي تمّام .
صارتْ بيروتَ و يافا ،
جرحاً عربياً في مدن الابداع
منذوراً للحب
ومسكوناً بالنار
صارت عشتار

266

Elegy to Khalil Hawi

I

As the poet waited
Aisha died in exile.
She became a morning star:
Lara and Khuzama/Hind and Safa'
Queen of queens
A Canaanite statue
A flame of a fire in the oil towers
And in the verses of the Song of Songs,
Blood upon the lines of the Torah
And upon the foreheads of the thieves of the revolutions.
She became the Nile and Euphrates
Vows of the poor
Over the Atlas Mountains
A lyric in the poetry of Abu Tammam.
She became Beirut and Jaffa
An Arab wound in the cities of creativity
Vowed for love
Possessed by fire
She became Ishtar.

حين ارتحل الشاعرُ
رسمت خارطةَ الأشياء خُطاهُ

حين انتحر الشاعرُ
بدأت رحلته الكبرى واشتعلت في البحر رؤاهُ
وحين اخترقت صيحتُهُ ملكوتَ المنفى
طفق الشعبُ القادمُ من صحراء الحبِ
يُحطم آلهة الطين
و يبني مملكة الله

□   □   □

II

As the poet departed
His footsteps drew the map of things.

III

When the poet killed himself
His great journey began
His visions burned in the sea.
When his cry penetrated the kingdom of exile
The people coming from the desert of love began
To smash the gods of clay
And build the Kingdom of God.

* * *

من أوراق عائشة

قالتْ : سأقتلُهُ
وأحمل رأسه لقبيلتي
صنماً ، لتعبدَهُ
وتحرقهُ ، إذا اقتتلتْ
وفي الصحراء أبني معبداً للحبِ
يحمل اسمه
تأوي إليه الطير ، في زمن المجاعةِ
أرتدي الأسمالَ
أعقر ناقتي
في باب معبده أنوخ
قالتْ : سأحملُهُ
إذا مرتْ عصورٌ
خاتماً في اصبعي
وأنوح في جوف الضريحْ

□   □   □

From the Papers of Aisha

She said: I will kill him
And carry his head to my tribe,
An idol to worship,
And to burn when they fight.
In the desert
I build a temple for love
In his name
The birds seek refuge
At the time of hunger
I wear tatters
I slaughter my camel
At the door of his temple I lament.
She said: I will carry him
A ring on my finger
If years pass
I will weep and mourn inside the grave.

* * *

ورقـة أخـرى

قالتْ : سأشنقهُ
بليلِ ضفائري
مهمَا أطلتُ الانتظارْ
وأعيدهُ حجراً على درب القوافلِ
سدرة / شيحاً وقيصوماً
وزهرة جلنارْ
قالت : سأغرس رمحه المسموم
في عـينيهِ
حتى لايرى ضوء النهارْ
وبكتْ وطال بها الوقوف على الطلول البالياتْ
واستنجدتْ بالساحرات
لتعيده حياً ،
ولكن الرياح السافيات
عفّت على آثار أقدام الطريد
وأدرك الليل النهار

□   □   □

Another Paper

She said: I will hang him
With the night of my tresses
No matter what, I waited.
And I will return him: a stone on the caravan roads
A lotus tree / a delicate bush
And a pomegranate blossom.
She said: I will plant his poisonous javelin
In his eyes
So he does not see the light of day.
She cried
And stood for a long time on the decayed ruins
Appealing to the enchantresses
To return him alive.
But the dusty winds
Erased the footprints of the hunted
And the night overtook the day.

* * *

نار الشعر

ـ ١ ـ

قالتْ : «ستموتُ غداً ، مسموماً في المنفى
أو مذبوحاً في سكين صديق أو مُخبر سلطانْ»
قال مخنثُ بابلَ : « أنت الآنْ
مأسورٌ ، باسم الشعراء الخصيان »
لكني ، كنتُ أموت غريقاً
في النور القادم، من أبعد نجمٍ ، محترقاً
في نار الشعر الزرقاء
أشحذ أسلحتي ، وأداعب في موتي ، القيثار

ـ ٢ ـ

كان يموتُ ببطء و يناضل ضد الحُلم المأجورْ
كان شهيد النور .
كان يقاتل في يافا / البصرة / بيروتْ
وعلى بوابةِ «كردستان» وشط العرب المسحور يموتْ

The Fire of Poetry

I

She said, "You will die tomorrow, poisoned in exile,
slaughtered by the knife of a friend
or a spy of the sultan."
The gay man of Babel said: "You are now
captive in the name of the castrated poets."
I was drowning to death
In the light coming from the farthest star
Burning
In the blue fire of poetry
Sharpening my weapons
Playing the lyre
In my death.

II

Struggling against a commissioned dream
Slowly he was dying
Martyr of the light
Fighting in Jaffa / Basra / Beirut
And at the gate of Kurdistan and the enchanted Shatt al Arab
He dies.

‑ ٣ ‑

كان يشاهد أشباه رجال ومخانيثَ وراء مكاتبهم يزنونْ
كان الوطن العربي القابع تحت الأنقاض يشاهدهم
في عين المأخوذ
يحصون القتلى من خلف مكاتبهم
يرنونْ
بعيون لصوص الديجور

‑ ٤ ‑

كان الشعب العربي يشاهد من تحت الأنقاضِ
نهايةَ عصر شهود الزورْ

‑ ٥ ‑

كان شهيدَ الوطن الصاعد من قاع الابداع غريقاً في النورْ

□   □   □

III

He witnessed half-men and homosexuals
Fornicating behind their desks.
The Arab World, sitting in destruction
Dazed, watching them counting those killed
From behind their desks.
Looking
With eyes of the thieves of darkness.

IV

From under the destruction
The Arab people were watching
The end of the era of false witnesses.

V

The martyr of the nation,
Ascending from the bottom of creativity
Was drowning in the light.

* * *

النقاد الأدعياء

جرذانُ حقولِ الكلماتْ
دفنوا رأسَ الشاعرِ في حقل رماذٍ
لكنّ الشاعرَ فوق صليب المنفى
حمل الشمسَ وطارْ

□   □   □

الولادة في مدن لم تُولَدْ

أولدُ في مدن لم تُولَدْ
لكني في ليل خريف المدن العربية
ــ مكسورَ القلب ــ أموتْ
أدفن في غرناطةَ حبي
وأقولُ :
« لا غالب إلا الحبُّ »
وأحرق شعري وأموتْ
وعلى أرصفة المنفى
أنهضُ من بعد الموت
لأ ولد في مدن لم تُولَدْ وأموتْ

□   □   □

False Critics

The rats of the fields of words
Buried the head of the poet
In a field of ashes
But the poet on the cross of exile
Carried the sun and flew.

* * *

The Birth in Unborn Cities

I am born in unborn cities
But in the night of the autumn of the Arab cities
Broken hearted I die.
I bury my love in Granada
I say:
"Nothing is victorious except love"
I burn my poetry and die.
On the sidewalks of exile
I arise after death
To be born in unborn cities
And to die.

* * *

المغني الأعمى

مطرٌ يتساقط فوق مساجد طهرانْ
مطر ونعاسْ
وسحابة خوف تجتاح الناسْ
لكنّ مغني الموت الأعمى
كان يغني للموتى العميانْ

□   □   □

راقصة الدخان

راقصةٌ من بحر الصينْ
ترقص في صندوق خزفيٍ
تُغمضُ عينيها
تبكي
ممسكةً في يدها عصفورْ
ترفعهُ قرباناً للنورْ
تقطف في يدها الأخرى زهرةَ لوزٍ
تخفيها في قاع الصندوق
تسقط مثل النجمة في بحر الصينْ
تتلاشى مثل دخان في الريحْ

□   □   □

The Blind Singer

Rain, falling over the mosques of Teheran
Rain and sleepiness
A cloud of fear sweeps over the people
But the blind singer of death
Was singing for the blind dead.

* * *

A Smoke Dancer

A dancer from the China Sea
Dances inside a porcelain box
She closes her eyes
She cries
Holding a bird in her hand
Raising it as a sacrifice to the light
In her other hand she picks an almond flower
Hiding it in the bottom of the box.
She falls like a star in the China Sea
She vanishes like smoke in the wind.

* * *

الولادة

الابداعُ هو الحبْ
والحبُ هو الموتْ
والابداع / الحب / الموت : ولادةٌ
فلماذا مات ، إذن، نيرودا / حكمتْ ؟
ولماذا آخر وردةٍ
في شرفة بيتي احترقتْ ؟
ولماذا نجمةُ حبي أفَلَتْ ؟

◻   ◻   ◻

بستان عائشة

بستانُ عائشة على «الخابور»
كان مدينةً مسحورة
عرب الشمالْ
يتطلعون إلى قلاع حصونها
و يواصلون البحث عن أبوابها
و يقدمون ضحيةً للنهر في فصل الربيع
لعل أبواب المدينةِ
تستجيب لهُمْ
فَتُفْتَحُ / كلما داروا

The Birth

Creativity is love
Love is death
Creativity / love / death: a birth
Why did Neruda and Hikmat die then?
Why is the last rose
In the window of my house burned?
And why has the star of my love
Vanished?

* * *

Aisha's Orchard

Aisha's orchard on the Khabur River
Was an enchanted city
The Arabs of the north
Gazing upon its castle
Ever searching for its gates
Offering a sacrifice to the river every spring
Perhaps the gates of the city
Respond to them
And open
Every time they turn

اختفى البستانُ
واختفت الحصونْ
فاذا خبا نجمُ الصباح
عادوا إلى «حلب» لينتظروا
و يبكوا ألف عام
فلعلهم في رحلة أخرى إلى « الخابور »
يفتتحونها
ولعلهم لايُفلحون
فالموت عرّافُ المدينةِ
هادمُ اللذاتِ
يعرف وحدهُ
أين اختفى بستان عائشةٍ
وفي أي العصور.

□   □   □

The orchard disappeared
And the castles disappeared.
When the morning star faded
They returned to Aleppo
To wait
And to cry for a thousand years
Perhaps in a future trip to the Khabur River
They will open the gates
And perhaps they will not.
Death is the fortune teller of the city,
The destroyer of pleasure
It alone knows
Where Aisha's orchard disappeared
And in which era.

* * *

صورة جانبية لعائشة

تُخفي وراء قناعها وجة الملاك
وملامح الأنثى
التي نضجت على نار القصائدِ
أيقظت شهواتها ريحُ الشمال
فتجوهرتْ تفاحةً / خمراً
رغيفاً ساخناً
في معبد الحب المقدّس
أدمنت طيب العناقْ
ظهرت بأحلامي ، فقلت : فراشة
رفّت بصيف طفولتي
قبل الأ وانْ
وتقمصت كل الوجوه
وسافرت / بدمي تنام
قديسةٌ تنسل في جوف الظلام
لتعانق الصنم المحطم
تنشب الأظفار في الحجر / الحطام
ياقوتةٌ / فَمُها / تشع طريةً /
نارُ الحقول /
ضفائرٌ معقودة /
عينان تضطرمان من فرط الحنان
وجه وراء قناعه ، يُخفي «مدائن صالح»
وحدائق الليمون في أعلى الفرات

Aisha's Profile

She hides behind her mask, the face of an angel
And the features of a woman
Ripened on the fire of poems.
The winds of the north awakened her desires
She changed into an apple / wine
A hot loaf of bread
In the temple of holy love
She became addicted to the pleasant embrace.
She appeared in my dreams, I said: A butterfly
Fluttering in the summer of my childhood
Premature
She incarnated all faces
And travelled / sleeping in my blood
A saint fleeing in the middle of the darkness
To embrace the shattered idol
She digs her fingernails in the stone / the rubble
Her mouth / ruby / fresh beams radiating
The fire of the fields
The braided tresses
Eyes burning from excessive compassion
A face behind its mask, hiding
The cities of Salih
And the lemon orchards of the Upper Euphrates

أمضيتُ صيف طفولتي
فيها ، وأدركني الشتاء
وحملت في منفاي بعد رحيلها
ذهبَ القصائد والرماد

□ □ □

الخائنـــة

كانت ، على منوالها ، ثلاثة تخونْ :
حبيبها ونفسها و بعلها المسكين
وعندما تحدج في مرآتها
ترى على صفحتها خائنةَ العيونْ

□ □ □

الوجـــه

وجهك في المرآة : وجهانِ
فلا تكذبْ
فان الله °
يراك في المرآة

□ □ □

There I spent the summer of my childhood
The winter overtook me.
After her departure
I carried in my exile
The gold of poems and ashes.

* * *

The Deceiver

She was as usual betraying three:
Her lover, herself, her poor husband
When she looks in her mirror
She sees herself
Betrayed by her eyes,
Herself, the deceiver.

* * *

The Face

Your face in the mirror: two faces
Do not lie
God
Sees you in the mirror.

* * *

سور الصين

تكسرت نصالهم فوق جدار سره الدفين
قالوا : انتهى !
وحفروا قبراً له
وسملوا عينيه بالسكينْ
لكنه ، كان على صليبهِ مُعلقاً
تضيئهُ البروق في ليل المنافي مثل سور الصين

□   □   □

امـــرأة

تعود كل ليلةٍ من قبرها النائي
إلى مدائن الصفيح
تمارس الحب مع الشيطان في بيوتها
تصهل مثل فرس في الريح
وكلما أدركها النعاس في تجوالها
عادت إلى الضريح

□   □   □

The Great Wall of China

Their blades were broken over the wall of its deep secret
They said: He is finished!
They dug a grave for him
And gouged out his eyes with a knife
He was hung upon his cross
Illuminated by the lightning in the nights of exile
Like the Great Wall of China.

* * *

A Woman

She returns every night from her distant grave
To the slums
Making love with the devil
In her houses
Neighing like a horse in the wind
When sleepiness grasps her in her wandering
She returns to her grave.

* * *

البصرة

ـ ١ ـ

كانت ، كعادة ، أهلها البسطاء
تجترح البطولة والفداء
تستقطر التاريخ معجزة
وشارات انتصار
و بوجهها العربي
في كل العصور
ـ مدينة الشعراء والعلماء ـ
قاومت الغزاة
و بأكرم الشجر النخيل
وشطها
كانت إلى الشهداء في معراجهم
زاد المعاد :
الشعر سر شبابها
و بطولة البشر / البناة

ـ ٢ ـ

خصلات شعرك في مرايا البحرِ :
نافذة وعصفور يطيرُ
ووردتان

Al-Basra

I

She was like the tradition of her simple people
Gaining heroism and sacrifice
Squeezing history to produce a miracle
And signs of victory.
With her Arab face
In all ages
This city of poets, of scholars
Resisted the invaders
With the most generous trees, the palms
And her shore
She was the journey to heaven for the martyrs.
The secret of her youth: poetry
And the heroism of her people / the founders.

II

The wisps of your hair in the mirrors of the sea:
A window and a flying sparrow
And two roses

وأنا المسافر في الزمان وفي المكانِ
وفي منافي الأبجدية والعروض
لغتي بضوئك أورقت
صارت قناديل المحبةِ
أزهرتْ
صارت منازل للقلوب
صار الزمان حديقةً
والبحر مرآة الحديقة والزمان

— ٣ —

كانت بلادي ترتدي ثوب الربيع
أوقفت راحلتي
وقلتُ : بكم تبيعْ
سلطانتي
هذا الضياء الأزرق الورديِّ
هذا الثوبَ
هذا الياسمينْ
قالت : « بكل قصائد الشعراء »
ضاحكةً
« ولكن ، لن أبيع ! »

□   □   □

I am the traveller in time and space
And in the exiles of the alphabets and the metrics
My language with your light put forth leaves
It became candlesticks of love
It flourished
It became houses for the hearts
Time became a garden
The sea a mirror of the garden and the time.

III

My country was wearing the spring dress
I stopped my camel
And said: My sultaness,
For how much will you sell
This rosy-blue glow,
This dress,
This jasmine?
She said, laughing: For all the poems of the poets
But I won't sell.

* * *

الرجل المجهول

رجل من بين غبار السنواتْ
طرق الباب
حيّاني ، قلت له : « أهلاً ! »
لكن الرجل المجهول ، قبالة ، بابي ، مات

□   □   □

الطاووس

مدن بالطاعون تموت وأخرى يضرب بها الزلزالْ
ومجاعات وحروب في كل مكان ودمار
وحضارات وعصور تنهار
لكنّ الطاووس ، بلا خجلٍ ، يُظهر عورته للناسْ

□   □   □

The Unknown Man

A man from among the dust of the years
Knocked at my door
He greeted me, I told him, "Welcome."
But the unknown man in front of my door died.

* * *

The Peacock

Cities die in plagues
Others are flattened by earthquakes
Everywhere starvation, wars and destruction
Civilizations, eras collapse.
But the peacock shamelessly
Shows his genitals to the people.

* * *

القصيدة

يتجول في نومي رجلُ النورْ
يتوقف في الركن المهجور
يُخرج من ذاكرتي ، كلماتٍ
يكتبها
ويُعيد كتابتها في صوت مسموع
يمحو بعض سطور
ينظر في مرآة البيت الغارق بالظلمة والنور
يتذكر شيئاً
فيغادر نومي
أستيقظ مذعوراً
وأحاول أن أتذكر شيئاً
مما قال وما هو مكتوب
عبثاً، فالنور
مسح الأوراق وذاكرتي
ببياض الفجر المقتول

□   □   □

The Poem

In my sleep the man of light wanders
He stops in the abandoned corner
He takes out words from my memory
He writes them
He rewrites them out loud
He erases some lines
He looks in the mirror of the house
Which is sinking in darkness and light.
He remembers something
He leaves my sleep
I wake up terrified
I try to remember something
He wrote and said.
In vain
The light
Erased the papers and my memory
With the whiteness of the dead dawn.

* * *

رجل وامرأة

يسقط الثلج على مدخنة البيتِ
وفي بهو المرايا
امرأة منتظرةٌ
رجل في دمها ، يحرث ، مأخوذاً
حقولَ الجسد المزدهرة
رجل يُولد من أضلاعها
يسكن فيها
يختفي في الذاكرة
نابضاً في قطرات دمها المفترسةِ
صاعداً كالشجرةِ
في خلاياها وفي أوصالها المرتجفة
رجل عانقها
فاشتعلت في دمها ، نارُ الفصول الأربعةُ

□   □   □

A Man and a Woman

The snow falls on the chimney of the house
In the hall of mirrors
A woman is waiting for
A man in her blood to plow
The fields of her flourishing body
For a man to be born from her ribs
To live in her,
To hide in her memory.
Throbbing in the ravishing drops of her blood
Ascending
Like a tree
In her cells
In her shivering limbs
A man embraces her.
The fire of the four seasons
Ignites in her blood.

* * *

صورة جانبية لمدينة ما

مقبرة تعلوها مقبرة ، بينهما
الحب / الموت / البشر الأحياء
والشحاذون وأهل اليُسر البخلاء
فاذا ما صحت بأعلى صوتكَ
عاد الصوت مليئاً بلهاث الموتى
وسعال شتاء السنوات
وإذا ما حاولت فراراً
طاردك الباعةُ والعيّارون الشـطّـار
في تلك المقبرة الكبرى
في تلك الطاحونةِ
في تلك الصحراء
نُحرتْ آلهة الشعرِ
ومات الشاعر في حانوت الخمّار

□　□　□

A Profile of a City

A cemetery above a cemetery, between them
Love / death / living humans
The beggars and the stingy wealthy people.
If you shouted in your loudest voice
The voice would return full of the gasps of the dead and
The coughs of the winter of the years.
If you attempted to flee
The vendors and the vagrants would chase you
In that big cemetery
In that mill
In that desert
Where the goddesses of poetry were slaughtered
And the poet died in the tavern.

* * *

سر النــار

في آخر يوم ، قبّـلتُ يديها
عينيها / شفتيها
قلتُ لها : أنت ، الآنْ ،
ناضجةٌ مثل التفاحة
نصفك : امرأةٌ
والنصف الآخر ليس له وصفٌ
فالكلمات
تهرب مني
وأنا أهرب منها
وكلانا ينهار
لطفولة هذا الوجه القمحي
وهذا الجسد المشتعل الريان
أبتهلُ الآن
وأقرب وجهي
من هذا النبع الدافق ، ظمآنْ
في آخر يوم ، قلتُ لها :
أنتِ حريقُ الغاباتِ
وماء النهرِ
وسر النارْ
نصفك ليس له وصفٌ
والنصف الآخر : كاهنة في معبد عشتارْ

□   □   □

Secret of Fire

On the last day
I kissed her hands,
Her eyes / her lips.
I said to her: you are now
Ripe like an apple
Half of you: a woman
The other half: impossible to describe.
The words
Escaped me
And I escaped them
Both of us collapsed
Now I pray
For the childhood of this light face
And for this ripe, burning body
I bring my face closer
To this gushing spring,
Thirsty.
On the last day, I said to her:
You are the fire of the forests
The water of the river
The secret of the fire
Half of you can not be described
The other half: a priestess in the temple of Ishtar.

* * *

حديث الحجر

حجرٌ، قال لآخرْ:
لم أسعد بوجودي في هذا السور العاري
فمكاني هو قصر السلطان
قال الآخر: ياهذا
محكوم بالموت عليكَ
سواء كنت هنا أم في قصر السلطان
فغداً يُهدم هذا القصر
وهذا السورُ
بأمرٍ من حاشية السلطان
ليعيدوا اللعبة من أولها
و يعيدوا توزيع الأدوار

□   □   □

•••••

306

A Conversation of a Stone

A stone said to another:
I am not happy in this naked fence
My place is in the palace of the sultan.
The other said:
You are sentenced to death
Whether you are here or in the sultan's palace
Tomorrow this palace will be destroyed
As well this fence
By an order from the sultan's men
To repeat their game from the beginning
And to exchange their masks.

* * *

Glossary

Abu Tammam: Habib ibn Aws al-Ta'i (A.D. 788-846), one of the greatest poets of the Abbasid era.

Aisha: The main heroine in Al-Bayati's poetry.

Al-Arsuzi, Zaki: (1900-1968) A leading intellectual and exponent of Arab nationalism who died in Damascus.

Alberti, Rafael: (1902-1984) A Spanish poet and playwright who fled Spain during Franco's reign and returned from exile in 1977 after the dictator's death. Alberti's best known poems are those in *Sobre Los Angeles* (About Angels). His poems are abstract, difficult and often surrealistic.

Al-Atlas: A mountain system in northwest Africa, extending across Morocco, Algeria, and Tunisia. The highest peak is in Morocco.

Al-Attar, Farid al-Din: (1140-1230) A great Persian mystic and poet born in Nishapur.

Al-Basra: A city in southeast Iraq, located on Shatt al `Arab.

Al-Hallaj: Al Husayn ibn Mansour (A.D. 858-922), an Abbasid Sufi philosopher and poet, who spent years in Sufi solitude and later roamed the country extolling the virtues of asceticism. He established a Sufi order and disciples rapidly gathered around him. He was accused of heresy and ultimately was crucified, decapitated and burned. He was the author of *Al-Tawasin*.

Alhambra: The court of Muslim Spain located in Granada, known by this name because of its red brick structure. This great monument to the splendor of Arab civilization and art was built by Muhammad al-Ahmar in the thirteenth century. It was from Alhambra that the last Muslim Arab caliph left Spain at the end of the fifteenth century.

Al-Khabur: Two rivers in Iraq—the Small Khabur, a fork in the Tigris River and the Big Khabur, the largest fork in the Euphrates River which stretches 320 kilometers.

Al-Khayyam, Omar: (d. A.D. 1123) Persian poet, mathematician, and astronomer. Al-Khayyam is best known for *Al-Ruba'iyat*, his four-line poems which praise the pleasures of nature, love, and wine, and declare the poet's sadness for the uncertainty of the future. Al-Khayyam's poems were translated into English in the nineteenth century. He was born in Nishapur.

Al-Mi'raj: The spiritual voyage taken by the Prophet Muhammad described in the Qur'an.

Al-Tawasin: The only surviving book by Al-Hallaj. The title is composed of "Ta" and "Sin," letters which were sacred to Al-Hallaj because they referred to Taha and Yasin, the names of the Prophet Muhammad.

Arabs of the North: The Arabs of the first migrations to the Fertile Crescent during pre-Islamic times.

Arcadia: An ancient pastoral district of the central Peloponnesus in Greece. Arcadia is a symbol for any place of peace and simplicity.

Arwad: A small island along the Syrian coast facing the city of Tartus.

Barada: A river that flows through Damascus.

Book of the Dead: A book from ancient Egypt containing prayers and charms meant to help the soul in the afterworld.

Bukhara: A city in the Uzbek in southwestern USSR famous for its mosques and schools.

Caucasus Mountains: A mountain range located in the Caucasus region in southeastern USSR between the Black Sea and the Caspian Sea.

Cities of Salih: Ruins located in the valley of Al-Qura north of the city of Al-Medina in the northwestern area of the Arabian peninsula. This location was the homeland of the Thamud people who were mentioned in the Qur'an.

Delphi: A city in ancient Greece at the foot of the Parnassus Mountains. A famous temple in this city housed a prophetess.

Garcia Lorca, Federico: (1899-1936) A famous Spanish poet and playwright who was brutally killed by Franco's fascist forces at the beginning of the Spanish Civil War.

Granada: The city in southern Spain where the famous Alhambra is found. It was the capital of the last Muslim Kingdom in Spain until 1492.

Great Bear: The constellation Ursa Major; its seven brightest stars form the Big Dipper.

Hawi, Khalil: A leading Arab poet born in Lebanon in 1925 who committed suicide following the Israeli invasion of Lebanon in 1982.

Helen: The beautiful wife of Menelaus, King of Sparta; the Trojan War was started because of her abduction by Paris to Troy.

Hikmet, Nazim: (1902-1963) One of the first Turkish writers to achieve an international reputation. He was accused of influencing students toward communism and sentenced to 35 years in prison. He was released in 1951 when the world's intellectuals campaigned for his freedom. Hikmet befriended Al-Bayati in 1958 while they were both living in the Soviet Union.

Hira': A mountain located northeast of Mecca known also as "the mountain of light." The prophet Muhammad hid in a cave on the mountain during his flight to Medina. A spider is said to have miraculously woven a web at the mouth of the cave to dissuade the Prophet's enemies from entering to look for him since they thought that the cave had been long abandoned.

Ibn `Arabi, Muhyi al-Din: (A.D. 1165-1240) A great philosopher and mystic poet who was born in Andalusia and travelled widely throughout North Africa and the Middle East. He died in Damascus and is entombed beneath a mosque named after him in the Al-Salihiya neighborhood at the foot of Qasyun Mountain. He loved Al-Nizam (Eye of the Sun), to whom his volume of poetry *Turjuman al-Ashwaq* (Translation of Desires) is dedicated.

Ishtar: The Babylonian and Assyrian goddess of love and fertility; the counterpart to the Phoenician Astarte.

Jinn: Supernatural beings that can take human or nonhuman form and influence human affairs.

Ka`bah: The sacred Muslim shrine at Mecca, toward which believers turn when praying. It contains the black stone given to Ibrahim by the angel Gabriel.

Kurdistan: A mountainous region in southwest Asia inhabited chiefly by Kurds, covering southeast Turkey, northern Iraq, and northwest Iran.

La`bi, Abdelatif: A Moroccan poet born in Fes in 1942. He was a political prisoner in Morocco from 1972 until 1980, when a worldwide campaign succeeded in gaining his freedom along with the freedom of an additional 89 political prisoners. He left Morocco for France in 1985.

Lady of the Seven Moons: A legendary woman who was worshipped by the inhabitants of the Black Sea area.

Machado Ruiz, Antonio: (1875-1939) The best-known Spanish poet of the "Generation of 1898," a period in Spanish letters characterized by intellectual crisis. He fled Spain during the Spanish Civil War and died in France.

Netocres: The name of an Egyptian/Babylonian princess, the counterpart of Ishtar and Aisha.

Neruda, Pablo: (1904-1973) A Chilean parliamentarian and diplomat, Pablo Neruda was one of the extraordinary political and visionary poets of the twentieth century. His poetry is rich, inventive and full of dramatic energy. Neruda was the recipient of the Nobel Prize for literature in 1971.

Ninevah: Capital of ancient Assyria, on the Tigris, opposite modern Mosul in northern Iraq.

Nishapur: A town in northeastern Iran which was one of the greatest Islamic cities in the Middle Ages. The birthplace of Omar Al-Khayyam and Farid Al-Din Al-Attar.

Papyrus: A writing material made from a plant by the ancient Egyptians, Greeks, and Romans.

Phoenix: A beautiful, lone bird which lived in the Arabian desert for five or six hundred years and then consumed itself in fire, rising renewed from the ashes to start another long life. A symbol of immortality.

Qasyun: A mountain overlooking Damascus, Syria.

Sayf al-Dawlah: `Ali ibn `Abdullah (A.D. 915-965), a famous Hamdani emir who reigned in Aleppo and was distinguished by his struggles against the Byzantines.

Seven Gates: The number seven is a magical number in the beliefs of all peoples of the ancient world, including the Sumerians, Babylonians, and Greeks. The seven gates of the world is the magical entrance for adventure and humanistic experience.

Shatt al-`Arab: A river in southeastern Iraq, formed by the confluence of the Tigris and Euphrates rivers and flowing southeast into the Gulf for 185 kilometers.

Shiraz: A city in south central Iran. It was called the city of the poets and saints.

Sinbad: A merchant sailor in *The Arabian Nights* who makes seven adventurous voyages.

Taurus Mountains: A mountain range along the southern coast of Asia Minor. The highest peak is in Turkey.

Thebes: An ancient city on the Nile in southern Egypt on the site of modern Luxor and Karnak.

Thief of Fire: The Greek god Prometheus who stole fire from the gods for the benefit of men on earth. After angering Zeus, he was chained to a rock and tortured for thousands of years until Hercules set him free.

Toledo: A city near Madrid in the center of Spain which was conquered by Tariq ibn Ziyad in A.D 714. King Alfonso of Spain recaptured the city in A.D. 1085.

Turkestan: A region in Central Asia extending from the Caspian Sea to the Gobi Desert, inhabited by Turkic-speaking peoples.

Valley of the Kings: A valley in southern Egypt where the Pharoahs were buried.

Waddah of Yemen: `Abdul Rahman ibn Isma`il, a man of great beauty who lived in Umayyad times during the rule of Caliph Al-Walid ibn `Abd al-Malik. He didn't go out in public unless he was veiled for fear of the evil eye and covetous women. According to legend, the Caliph's wife fell in love with him and during one of his secret visits, she was forced to hide him in a box. The Caliph was told by his men that Waddah was hidden in the box and he had Waddah buried inside it in A.D. 708.

Zapata, Emiliano: (1879-1919) A Mexican revolutionary and politician who called for agricultural reform and was assassinated.

Zarathustra: A Persian prophet who lived in the sixth or seventh century B.C. and founded the Zoroastrian religion.